PRAISES FOR

"In *Illegitimate*, Christa Armstead examines the devastating impacts of classism, racism, sexism, abandonment, and abuse of power. Her emotional story offers authentic truth telling, delivering a memoir that will break your heart and put it together again. In the end, readers will cheer as she overcomes significant hardships to discover healing, love, and deep faith—a drastic contrast to the religious hypocrisy that wrecked her childhood family."

~Julie Cantrell, New York Times *and* USA Today *bestselling author of* Perennials.

"*Illegitimate* is the journey many have started, and some have accomplished. *Illegitimate* is more than a search-and-discover mission. It answers many plights that have attacked and ravaged the nation and the world. This wonderful, heart-wrenching, and moving truth journal addresses the unspoken truths of the damage and residue of pain and suffering that the clergy does not want to address."

~Earl A. Smith, Sr., *Team Pastor,* San Francisco 49ers and Golden State Warriors

"This book is indeed a must read! Christa Armstead's story is a missing puzzle piece of healing, empowerment, and transformation that will fill a space many carry within their souls. Through her deep transparency she provides a road map for moving from pain to purpose, trauma to testimony, and from isolation to empowerment. Let this book bless you through whatever challenges you're facing."

~*Dr. Efrem Smith, Co-Lead Pastor of Midtown Church, author of* Killing Us Softly *and* The Post Black and Post White Church

"Christa Armstead was born a poster child for religious hypocrisy. Her story of wrestling redemption from poverty and hopelessness, using the power of her faith to find a life path of love, creating a family guided by her contagious energy, and upending preconceived notions of what's possible, is uplifting to anyone hoping to reorient their lives and use their God-given gifts to find peace."

~*Ann Kreis, Trustee Emeritus Berklee College of Music, Harvard Business School*

ILLEGITIMATE

MEMOIR OF A PRIEST'S DAUGHTER

ILLEGITIMATE

MEMOIR OF A PRIEST'S DAUGHTER

CHRISTA ARMSTEAD

*Authentic truth-telling
...that will break your heart
and put it back together again.*

Julie Cantrell
New York Times and USA Today best-selling author of *Perennials*

REDEMPTION PRESS

Published by Redemption Press, PO Box 427, Enumclaw, WA 98022. Toll-Free (844) 2REDEEM (273-3336)

Redemption Press is honored to present this title in partnership with the author. The views expressed or implied in this work are those of the author. Redemption Press provides our imprint seal representing design excellence, creative content, and high-quality production.

Cover design and Author's photo by Kira Bautista.

Erik Armstead family photo and 49ers photo provided by 49ers Media Team. All rights reserved.

ISBN 13: 978-1-64645-547-8 (Soft)
           978-1-951310-58-5 (ePub)
Library of Congress Catalog Card Number: 2023908394

DEDICATION

For my Aunt Fern and Aunt Vicky. If it weren't for you two,
I might not be here today. Thank you for your sacrifices.

To my husband Guss and to my children,
Aaron, Armond, Alexis, and Arik
Thank you for always believing in me.

To my best friend Valorie—
Thank you for encouraging me to write my story and
for all the hours you spent editing the first draft.

A Note to Readers

*ILLEGITIMATE… is a true account of the author's life.
The stories and events she shares in this memoir are her recollections
from important scenes of her life. Some names and events have been
modified to protect the privacy of family members.*

CONTENTS

1

PRIME TIME TV

The TV studio lights shone bright and hot from all angles on Mama and me, along with the lineup of other women seated with us on the stage. An enormous camera zoomed in as Phil Donahue deftly sidled up to the audience, microphone in hand.

"I'd like to introduce our first guests," he crooned in his familiar fatherly tone. "Diane and her daughter." Lifting a presentational hand in my direction, he beamed at the audience. "Isn't she gorgeous?"

While they nodded and cooed in agreement, I shifted uneasily in my seat.

"Diane." Serious now, Mr. Donahue addressed Mama. "This is your daughter, Christa, whose father . . ." He paused, presumably to add to the impact of what he was about to reveal. ". . . is a Catholic priest."

Instantly, the audience's smiles turned to open-mouthed stares. This was not something people talked about in 1986, and certainly not on daytime television. Their reaction stunned me. If these strangers found our family secret this shocking, how would people who actually knew me react?

Unlike me, my mother didn't seem bothered. She said, matter-of-factly, "Correct."

Mr. Donahue leaned in and lowered his voice, as if he were sharing a juicy piece of gossip with friends at a party. "I assume he still *is?*"

"No," Mama said. "The church would not tell me, but at some point, he left the priesthood, and we spent a lot of time and energy trying to find him. Today, he's not a priest. He's a high school teacher and therapist."

To this, Mr. Donahue raised his brows, and the entire audience released a rush of nervous laughter.

I wanted to disappear.

"So, you have *found* him." Mr. Donahue pushed Mama for more. "And he acknowledges that he is the father?"

The audience seemed spellbound. I could sense he was enjoying the building tension, with my life as the bait he dangled before them. As if he were saying, *You think that's something? Wait until you hear what comes next!*

Of course, Mama delivered. "In a court of law, when she was seventeen years old . . . about three weeks before she turned seventeen . . . he finally signed the papers stating that he was the father."

Mr. Donahue muttered under his breath, adding a dramatic and well-placed, "Um-hum . . ."

Taking her cue, Mama went on. "He fought this all along. Denied it. He said, 'You can't touch me, so until you find the money to go into court and prove this, I'm scot-free.'"

I sat still and quiet the entire time, keeping my head down and choking back tears as Mama told the entire world my greatest shame.

My father was not only a priest; he was a man who had denied being my father . . . even after all these years.

"He's a successful man." Mr. Donahue went on. "Did I read where you estimate his salary to be about fifty thousand?"

"Yes," Mama said. "That is the salary figure he gave the DA."

"He's also married, with his own children."

Mama nodded. "He has one daughter."

"Twenty years ago. Well, you've got to tell us how old you are."

"I don't mind telling you. I'm thirty-nine today, but I was fourteen when I first met him."

Mama didn't so much as pause when the audience gasped and murmured at the news.

"Initially, he was just my priest and my confessor. And then a couple years later, he became my religion instructor, and then he became my therapist, and he started visiting my home, just like . . ." She pointed down the line of women seated with us. ". . . my story is very similar to Dee's." Mama eyed one of the other women, whose story of predatory grooming mirrored her own.

"So, he became a friend of the family. Like Dee, it was a situation whereby he took a lot of personal interest in me. I was an honor student in a special elite school, and he really made me feel I could be something. I could achieve something. I could go on to college. No adult figure had ever shown me this type of attention."

We wouldn't know until seeing the show air that at this moment, a caption flashed on the screen:

Diane had a sexual relationship with a priest.

I would erupt when I learned that news, discovering they'd captioned it in a way that could have implied that the sexual predator was my mother!

Unaware of the caption at the time, Mama continued. "He made sure that I was chosen for special awards in school, special privileges, and academic attention."

The camera scanned the studio audience, and I followed its focus to find an older woman looking on intently with a scrutinizing glower, holding her hand to her face. Another woman about three rows back sat with her eyes tightly closed but unable to keep the tears from rolling down her face. *What had been her experience?*

It seemed clear that some of the audience members were angry at us. Their tight-lipped expressions said it all. *This woman has no business desecrating the Holy Church with these lies. What kind of person would have sex with her priest? A priest fathering a baby!? Scandalous!*

Eventually, the camera returned to Mr. Donahue, who was already prompting Mama for more, ramping up the shock value at every turn. "So, this man is White?"

Mama nodded. "Only three Black females in the entire school. Very elite . . . where the mayor's daughter would attend. You have to pass a test to be admitted into the school—quite an honor and achievement, especially for a Black student, to be enrolled in this particular private school. Because there were only three of us, I was highly visible in the school."

"Do I understand that you were able to extract child support from this person for a year and a half?"

"Not a year and a half. It was only for three to four months . . . until she turned eighteen."

I slouched lower in my seat, wishing this would end. I'd spent my entire life burying these painful secrets. Why did Mama find it necessary to expose us on TV like this?

"So . . ." Mr. Donahue leaned in. "His obligation to child support expired, and if I'm understanding our research now, you want retroactive child support for the first eighteen years of her life."

To my surprise, a few members of the audience applauded. This was what finally broke me, and I lowered my head again, unable to hide the fact that I was crying. I tried to wipe the tears away quickly, but the camera found me, and the world saw me at my most vulnerable.

"That is true, very true, not only for me, but for others." Mama explained. "That is why we asked Attorney Allred to take this case on." She gave a quick nod to Gloria, who sat on my other side. "We are trying to establish legal precedent to change all the child support laws. I went to the DA office when my daughter was first born for help. Father Chris had told me to go on welfare, go into a home for unwed mothers, and put the baby up for adoption, so no one would ever know."

I was crying harder now. *If only I could disappear!*

Mama and Gloria both reached out and grabbed my hands. If the audience hadn't been watching me before that moment, all eyes were now on me.

"The welfare department had to do an investigation. They'd dropped it because he was a priest."

But Mama's words weren't grabbing the audience's attention anymore. Mr. Donahue followed their focus, turning his questions my way.

"Christa, uh . . . you can take your time here. If you want to pull yourself together you can certainly do so." He paused for a second or two and then said, "You're crying. Why?"

I couldn't find words to explain, so he spoke for me.

"You, uh . . . you feel victimized, and you feel your mother has been? How would you verbalize your own pain?"

It took all the courage I could muster, but I looked at Mr. Donahue and found my voice. "I feel very victimized. I feel it's unfair for him to try to hide out and then tell her that he was going to leave her with a child to support, knowing her situation. Knowing that I would grow up in deprived neighborhoods and that I would suffer because of it. With no moral conscience at all. He didn't think to himself that . . . that's a child, my child, and she's going to suffer."

Mr. Donahue seemed satisfied with my answer. Thankfully, he gave me a break, introducing Gloria as the camera panned out to show the entire panel of women, including our high-profile attorney.

When the audience applause quieted, Gloria spoke up. "These children are innocent victims." She patted my arm. "Like Christa. She's an innocent victim. Her life should not have been changed for the worse. We have to stand up and fight against injustice."

The emotions continued to flow as they moved on to each woman's story. One shared her ordeal of being molested in the church by multiple priests. Like my mother's experience, this abuse had been swept under the rug by the church for years, all while innocent victims were having their lives completely and utterly shattered, some never to recover. My mother had certainly never recovered from the breakdown she'd had when I was just a few months old, and for the first time, I was finally beginning to realize the depth of the pain she had carried.

How many times had my mother tried to talk about the night she broke? "Christa," she'd said to me, "I don't know whose care you were in on the night I went screaming down the street. When the police came and got me, they must have taken you somewhere safe? It's foggy and just too painful for me to go back there, honey. I'm so sorry you had to endure so much pain because of your father and me."

My mother had recounted this story to me on many occasions. But sitting on that stage, watching these women rally together to tell their secrets, I knew the things that had happened to Mama were too dark to talk about in their entirety.

That was when I finally began to realize that for my entire life, she had done the best she could do.

2

WHO'S THE FATHER?

The warm breeze of September 1, 1967, gently blew through the streets of Los Angeles, enveloping the city in a comforting embrace.

It had been nearly four years since the brutal assassination of John F. Kennedy, the progressive American president who lost his life for being a sympathizer to the civil rights movement. The militant-minded activist Malcom X was gunned down two years later, but despite daily death threats, the more peaceful Martin Luther King, Jr.—along with his counterparts at the Southern Christian Leadership Conference—continued to bring attention to the many racial injustices taking place across the nation.

Everyone seemed focused on the issues of the Black community, but no one knew the silent suffering of one African American teen in inner-city LA.

"It's time." A Mercy League social worker spoke softly to the young woman—Diane—who was about to become my mother.

The Mercy League was a charity-funded, two-hundred-bed home for unwed mothers. It served less as a place of support and encouragement than as a place to hide a pregnancy prior to an even-more-secretive adoption. Though the young residents shared morning sickness, contractions, and fear of labor, most didn't even know each other's last name.

With the urgency of a race car driver, the social worker transported my mother to Cedars Sinai Hospital. This was the ride the young mothers both anticipated and dreaded. It meant that, *Finally, the baby is coming!* It also meant that close friendships, forged in secrets and shame, would end abruptly.

For my mother, it also meant that the life she had made for herself would never be the same.

The Supremes' "Love is Here and Now You're Gone" looped in the dark recesses of my mama's mind, as she was admitted to the maternity ward. She was a mere stone's throw from the glitz and glamour of Hollywood, and yet a world apart from the luxurious life associated with that place.

Nine pounds and eight ounces lighter, Mama emerged from the foggy cloak of anesthesia. Alone in the sterile recovery room, she searched for proof of life. Right on cue, a shift nurse entered, pushing the nursery trolley.

There I was. Diane's little girl. I was swaddled and sleeping soundly, but Mama couldn't wait to hold me. She pulled me from the bassinet and unbundled my tiny form. Ten fingers. Ten toes. My chest rose softly as she inhaled. Her new-mother's heart surged with waves of relief, then grief.

She cuddled her baby close against her breast, making promises with her heart that only the infant could hear. Secretively, she gave me a piece of my father's name. *Surely, no one will connect the dots.* And for my middle name, well . . . she loved that Beatles song, "Michelle."

She whispered to me, "Wouldn't it be nice to have the Beatles sing a song, just for you?" She sang softly, "Christa Michelle, my belle."

While biracial marriage was only legal in some states, Diane had brought a beautiful redheaded baby from her womb; a baby who could clearly pass for White. Word of this anomaly—bordering on criminal and reeking of scintillating scandal—had already made its way around the ward.

The Cedars Sinai nurse raised a judgmental brow as she helped Mama—the chocolate-brown beauty—complete the birth certificate. Mama answered as she knew she shouldn't, confirming that yes, the father was *Caucasian*.

The nurse tried to piece together facts, shooting invasive questions like bullets, but Mama shifted her focus back to me and left the line next to "father's name" blank. She vowed to keep the truth a secret, and that was exactly what she did.

Until she didn't.

3

KEEPING SECRETS

Four years earlier Pacoima, California, a suburb of the San Fernando Valley, was known as one of the few neighborhoods to accept people of color. As a result, families flocked to the area to purchase a piece of the American dream. A brand-new three-bedroom home could be acquired for $63.26 a month—not cheap, but within reach of many hard-working Blacks.

The community's African American socialite, Mrs. Liz Holmes, wasn't typical by any means. She was a highly cultured world traveler who frequently accompanied her brother Paul, a champion prize fighter, during his trips to Europe. The civic leader, owner of Soul Sound Records, and twice-married mother of four, was known to throw A-list parties with fine food and abundant liquor. At the Holmes household, middle class for people of color never felt so good.

Mrs. Holmes . . . Liz . . . had no idea at the time, but in a few short years she would also be known as Meme. My grandmother.

From the outside looking in, perfection furnished each room. So, it was no surprise when Mrs. Holmes received a letter from the city's prestigious private Catholic school for girls. It read:

Dear Mrs. Holmes,
This letter is to inform you and your daughter Diane of her acceptance to Bishop Alemany High School. We are pleased to report that she has exceeded the academic requirements to begin her freshman year with us.

In His Service,
Bishop Alemany High School Registrar

Diane held the acceptance letter in her trembling fingers with a tingling mix of joy, apprehension, and vindication. The family's eldest and darkest, she finally had her ticket to redemption. Louder than any words, this letter conveyed that she would no longer be ignored or cast aside.

Her acceptance into Bishop Alemany raced past the color of her skin. It didn't even make a pit stop at her mother's grinding words of warning: "Diane, whatever you do, don't you dare be dating dark boys and bringing home dark babies."

The acceptance letter meant that, at roll call each morning, her mark of intelligence would be made. As would her worth. Yes, at Bishop Alemany High School, Diane would be surrounded by Whites—including some of the wealthiest and most prestigious politicians' children. While her younger sister, Vicky, would enter San Fernando Public High School the following year, Diane would prove that she was different not only because she was dark chocolate brown among such fairer-skinned, green-eyed siblings, but also because her academic prowess had made her an equal to the elite White students of her day.

Nevertheless, entry into the whiter world didn't go as smoothly as Diane hoped. Forging new friendships among her more affluent peers proved difficult. How could any of them relate to her experiences? They knew nothing of her father Joe's playboy antics. They had not endured her parents' earth-shattering divorce . . . a divorce that quickly led Liz to a rebound second marriage and another three children who didn't share Diane's last name. How could she explain her blended family, a situation that was rare in those days and stood in stark opposition to her classmates' seemingly stable lives?

Without friends, Diane survived the loneliness at school by focusing on her work and by clinging tightly to her faith. She'd always been deeply devoted to God and had even considered becoming a nun, riding her bike to Mass each Sunday to please her Heavenly Father.

But she inevitably grew tired of the isolation. She desperately needed to turn to someone other than God for companionship. Noticing her vulnerability, a priest, teacher, and therapist by the name of Father John Christenson stepped in as her mentor.

Father Chris, as he was known, was a patient man in his thirties, who became the first adult to really listen to Diane. He said he saw greatness in her. Who wouldn't? She was an articulate, intelligent student with a promising future. He convinced the teen there was no reason that anything should keep her from catapulting to the top of politics, medicine, law . . . whatever her heart desired.

Building her self-esteem, Father Chris recommended his young protégée for numerous awards and fueled her natural desires to succeed at all academia had to offer. He believed in her, and in time he helped her believe in herself.

Their Tuesday afternoon sessions, laced with safe boundaries and spiritual guidance, quickly became the highlight of Diane's week. Tucked within the confines of his private office, the teacher and student prayed together. In time, she grew to trust her older mentor, asking him just about anything concerning God; even sharing her more personal thoughts about becoming a nun. In Diane's company, Father Chris was down-to-earth and easy to talk to, and often put himself in the moment, making the lonely outsider feel as if she were the most important person in the world.

Diane admired Father Chris's kind qualities. She had great respect for his commitment—real heartfelt, lifetime devotion to God—that included his vow of poverty, chastity, and allegiance to the Catholic faith.

Finally, she'd found a friend! And with the absence of her own father in her life, she found security in the priest's fatherly mentorship.

Soon, Father Chris began ministering to Diane's family too, visiting Liz's home for dinner and complimenting the family matriarch for her daughter's many talents. The Holmes family felt privileged to have an ordained man of the cloth dining at their table, a visit tantamount to a blessing for the whole family.

Liz, beaming with pride for her eldest daughter's accomplishments, was finally feeling at ease about her decision to allow her to attend Bishop Alemany High School. While she'd certainly fought fears when her daughter chose to attend the mostly White school, the incredible opportunities now being afforded her were proof that things had gone as they should. She credited the priest with the positive changes occurring in her daughter. Since starting their weekly meetings, Diane seemed much happier.

On the surface, life was grand, and when Pacoima's civic committee welcomed its gifted African American student to compete in its annual beauty pageant, Father Chris was the first to encourage her entry. Diane's well-proportioned curves, wavy hair, and stunning blend of Native American and African American features made her a standout. Her success in the pageant became another boost to Diane's self-esteem.

***

But sometimes even counselors need counseling. And while Diane was thriving under the guidance of Father Chris, he was struggling with a temptation that was growing stronger than his faith.

Father Chris usually brought his life concerns to an experienced psychologist on campus, Dr. Smith. He felt safe divulging some of his darkest thoughts, the very perplexities that kept him awake at night, trusting that all was confidential. Topping the thirty-two-year-old's list was the occasional glass of liquor that warmed his insides and quieted his mind. He didn't necessarily enjoy drunkenness; relaxation was his goal. The means to get there, however, stood in opposition to the conditions of the collar.

In the comfort of such grace, Father Chris confessed his sins, minimizing any guilt or shame with Dr. Smith's, "God bless you, Father. You are, after all, human."

Until one afternoon, when the young priest rocked the session with a startling admission. "I'm questioning whether I should stay in the priesthood."

This was something altogether more serious than confessing a drinking problem. Yet, true to Dr. Smith's previous responses, the shocking admission was met with more empathy, support, and even encouragement as Father Chris was told yet again, "You're just a man, after all."

***

One day, as Diane sat in biology class, she received a mysterious note. Strange as it seemed, Dr. Smith, the on-campus psychologist, wanted to see her in his office. The moment the bell rang, she hurried to comply.

By the time she found herself seated across the desk from the imposing man, her stomach was in knots. She'd never before been summoned to see anyone on staff like this. What had she done wrong?

Eyeing her carefully, Dr. Smith steepled his hands in front of his face. "Diane." His voice hummed with practiced compassion. "It's been brought to my attention that someone has taken an interest in you."

She sat up a little straighter. So . . . she hadn't done anything wrong? Being a senior, she'd been keenly aware of her classmates looking into scholarships and job opportunities. But . . . why would news of something like that come from the psychologist?

Before she could question him, the man continued. "There's just one thing, and I can't overstate the importance of this." Lowering both his hands and his voice, he leaned forward, causing her to do the same. "You must keep what I'm about to tell you an absolute secret." Pointing a finger toward the ceiling, as if to imply that she was not even to discuss this with the good Lord, he added, "Tell no one."

Confused, she fingered the pleats of her plaid wool skirt. How on earth would she be able to tell anyone, when she had no idea what this was about?

Realizing that he was waiting for her to agree, she gave him a quick nod.

"Good." The corners of his mouth lifted as he relaxed deeper into his chair. "The times being what they are, I'm sure you'll understand the delicacy of this situation."

The *times?* "I'm sorry. . . I don't—"

"Normally"—he lifted a hand to silence her— "I wouldn't be asked to intervene in a situation that's *romantic* in nature. . ."

He kept talking, but at the word "romantic," she had stopped hearing. That was what this was about? Someone had taken an interest in her . . . *romantically?*

That seemed odd. Was it normal for someone to ask a school staff member to act as matchmaker with a student? Although female students at Bishop Alemany High School were kept separate from the boys, Diane, like most senior girls, dreamed of what it would be like to sock hop, soda pop, and jukebox with a handsome partner. What seventeen-year-old girl didn't?

By the time she recommenced listening, Dr. Smith was talking like this was perfectly normal, and even a little bit thrilling.

"Clandestine meetings are to be arranged, of course."

"I'm sorry, but . . ." She flipped through a mental list of unanswered questions and settled on, "Why?"

Arching an eyebrow as if her question had taken him by surprise, he reached for a pad of notepaper and a pen. As he shielded the paper with one hand, he began writing. "I assumed you'd understand my meaning, given that you're . . ." He glanced up from the paper long enough to give her a hasty once-over, then returned to his writing. "The man in question is White."

She caught her breath. So that was what he'd meant.

Clicking his pen, Dr. Smith tore the top slip of paper off the pad, then folded it and held it out to her. "Wait until you get home to read the identity of this person. I'll arrange for the two of you to meet, but in the meantime, remember; no one—not a schoolmate, faculty member, or even your own mother—can know. This is to remain a secret, between just the three of us."

Clumsily, Diane rose from the chair, clutching the paper in her fist, and gathered up the stack of schoolbooks she'd rested on the edge of his desk. Without another word, she scooted back out into the hallway.

Hugging her books to her chest, she made her way down the hall, past classmates and teachers who had no idea that she—Diane Holmes—wasn't the same girl she'd been just a few minutes before. She glanced down at the folded paper in her hand and smiled to herself. A secret romance; a forbidden love.

Bottom line: someone wanted to date her!

While secrecy seemed like a strange condition, it actually added to the romance. Besides, with a trusted adult like Dr. Smith making the arrangements, surely everything would be legitimate.

The weight of this news grew enormously as Diane's fellow classmates filed past her without a care in the world. *Who was this would-be suitor?*

Unable to stand the suspense for another second, she darted into the restroom, ignoring the couple of girls who stood at the mirror applying lipstick and gossiping. She hurried into a stall, latched the door, and closed her eyes.

A White boy. Could she allow her heart to go there, knowing that interracial relationships often brought hardship to all involved? Then the words of her mother returned to her, warning her not to be dating any "dark-skinned boys."

Maybe the racial difference was actually a good thing. Convinced that it was something she could handle, she opened her eyes and looked down as she unfolded the paper.

Her heart practically jumped out of her chest when she read the hastily scrawled name.

Tears pricked her eyes as it became clear that race wasn't the only difference they would need to overcome.

4

CAUTION
TO THE WIND

September 1966

On the afternoon of Diane's eighteenth birthday, sunshine and the cheerful twitter of birds filtered through the bathroom window. Smoothing her hair into a ponytail, she couldn't help but smile. The woman looking back at her in the mirror had her sights firmly set on continuing her education at Stanford with a major in literature.

Tackling college life at Stanford will be no problem.

After all, she had won her own academic marathon when she graduated early and with honors from Bishop Alemany High School. Father Chris had recommended her for several scholarships and often told her how bright and special she was.

The sky was the limit, both in her school career and her love life.

It had seemed strange at first, seeing Father Chris as more of an equal. She'd been resistant, but he'd agreed that it would be best to take things slowly. His willingness to only go as far as she felt comfortable allowed her to adjust. Little by little, day by day, she had begun to realize that their age difference really wasn't a big deal. He wasn't so different from her. And she already trusted him, after all the time they'd spent getting to know each other in the years they'd been acquainted.

Plus, he was a man of God. He wouldn't get involved in anything that wasn't pure, good, and right.

After a while, late-night phone calls and occasional stolen moments together were no longer enough. Diane became sure they were meant for each other. Despite her better judgment, she even began dreaming of the day when she would walk down the aisle and the two of them would finally be able to profess their love for one another out in the open.

With Father Chris's support, Diane had moved from her family home to a sorority house. He'd explained that the move would help ease her transition into college that fall, but it would also help her escape the tensions at home that had begun to spring up again between Diane and her mother.

While Diane had managed to keep the enhanced status of her relationship with Father Chris under wraps, her mother sensed the newfound self-confidence her daughter exuded. With it came an air of what felt to her mother like defiance, and she didn't approve.

Mrs. Holmes was not on board with her daughter being thrust into the university world at such a young age. When she confronted the house director with her concerns, Diane had been forced to move out of the sorority, which put her in a real bind. Angry, she'd refused to move back home with her mother. Where would she go?

A tiny, roach-infested one-bedroom apartment in Los Angeles would have to suffice until the doors of Stanford University opened for her in the fall. Then, maybe Father Chris could help her secure another room on campus.

As she put the finishing touches on her makeup, a knock on the apartment door sent her heart racing. Anticipating her birthday visitor, she gave herself one last assessing look, then hurried to the door. She swung it open to find Father Chris looking every bit the Hollywood heartthrob.

She caught her breath. Something about him was different. Then it dawned on her as she stepped aside to let him in.

"I've never seen you without your clergy collar."

***

To Father Chris, the forty-mile trip to visit the beautiful Diane on this very special day had taken no time at all. The borrowed rectory station wagon seemed to have steered itself directly to her front door that day.

The secrets he'd shared all those months ago with Dr. Smith about his growing longings for Diane had disarmed all rational thinking. And now that Diane had finally come of age, Dr. Smith had given Father Chris his blessing, reminding him again that he was *only human!*

Only human, indeed. As he entered Diane's apartment that afternoon, he thought his heart might beat right out of his chest. She was beautiful. And in that moment, she was his.

***

"Happy birthday, Diane."

Waiting till Diane had shut the door, Father Chris opened his arms, and she happily fell into his embrace. He had helped her in so many ways. She felt in her heart that she wouldn't have made it through the trials of teenage life, much less the angst at home, without this very special friend, a man who had become the most important person in her life. A trusted mentor. Who was becoming so much more.

Stepping out of the hug, she clutched his hand. "I'm so glad you're here!" She led him to the lumpy old sofa that was the only piece of furniture in what functioned as her living room. "Sit down. I made some iced tea."

As the afternoon wore on, they talked, laughed, and drank iced tea. Then, he began confiding in her. He confessed that he'd had his share of struggles—with drinking; with thoughts of abandoning his call; and with his undeniable feelings for her.

She edged closer to him on the sofa as he spilled his heart and confessed his love for her.

Almost blind to the less-than-ideal surroundings, which included noisy neighbors and constant traffic, there was nothing to keep him from hurtling toward the passion that had been building inside of him.

One kiss.

The vow was broken.

Diane, who wanted desperately to please God, hesitated at the threshold of becoming a priest's lover.

"But God is okay with our love, Diane." Father Chris assured her.

Those words melted her resolve long enough to change their lives forever.

5

BROKEN DREAMS

December 1967

A loud knock on Diane's apartment door nearly startled her out of her skin. Gingerly, she peered down at the tiny bundle she held and sighed, relieved that the sound hadn't awoken her.

Taking care not to wake the baby in her arms, she pulled herself up from the lumpy sofa and tiptoed across the small room. Cautiously, she peered through the peephole.

"Diane, it's me."

If it were possible to feel the warmth of the sun while standing in a rainstorm, this was how Diane felt when she saw Father Chris. Minus his clergy collar, he looked like any other man. A man who had chosen her. And—finally—chosen to return.

As she quickly checked her reflection in the window that served as a mirror, her mind raced to that horrible day more than a year ago. She'd given Chris the news of her condition, expecting him to be as shocked as she'd been at first. But once he'd accepted their reality, she'd fully anticipated a marriage proposal.

Instead, he'd broken out into a sweat, then paced the room, and stormed out. When he eventually returned, it was to tell her that he'd made arrangements for an adoption. When she'd flat-out refused, he'd abruptly left. She hadn't seen or heard from him since.

Now, swallowing a squeal of delight, she patted her hair into place, smiled, and exhaled for the first time in months.

But as she pulled the door open, her smile faded.

Chris stood there, his hair mussed, his shirt wrinkled and stained, and his eyes frightfully affixed to the bundle she held. Then, gazing cautiously through the doorway, he took in the laundry piled in a basket on the floor, the dirty dishes stacked next to the sink, and a slew of baby items scattered across the slum apartment.

"Well, don't just stand there, Chris." Relief at seeing him gave way to impatience. "Come in."

His feet moved him inside just about two feet from the threshold.

After hip-bumping the door shut, Diane stood in front of him, rocking their baby.

He wouldn't, or couldn't, speak. So, to break the tension, she pulled the faded pink blanket away from Christa's tiny face and angled her toward him.

Flinching, he quickly looked away.

"She's beautiful, isn't she?" Swallowing a threatening wave of panic, Diane shifted the baby to meet his gaze. "She's got your hair and . . ."

The shamed priest closed his eyes and whispered pointedly, "Why did you do this?"

Shrinking back, Diane could feel her dreams slipping through her fingers like sand. "We can still be together, Chris. A real family."

"No." He bit off the word, keeping his voice low as if not to disturb God.

"You're her *father*." Her voice caught on the word. "You won't even look at her."

"I *can't*, Diane." He shook his head. "You shouldn't have done this."

Her chest burned. Where did he get off, blaming *her*? "You said we could be together. You *promised* we would be together—"

"No, Diane." Finally, he looked her in the eye. "If you had given . . . *her* . . . up for adoption, we *could* be together. I had it all set up for you. Why didn't you do as I asked?"

"Are you really saying . . . Chris, I can't stay here. Look at this place! It's no place to raise a baby. I need your help."

"If you had followed the plan—"

"The plan? It was *your* plan. Look at our daughter, Chris. Look at her!" Diane's voice broke the whisper barrier and echoed throughout her dismal room.

At last, his eyes rested on Christa. His child.

"She's half White, Chris, and half Black. Don't you understand? I couldn't give her up because she won't belong anywhere. You know that. She can only belong with us. We have to do right by her." Diane's heart raced, and her tears soaked into the baby's blanket.

"This was never meant to be." His voice came out low and menacing. Then he turned his back on them and walked out of the apartment, not even pausing to say goodbye.

***

Alone.

Diane felt this five-letter word should be her new name. She wore it like a cloak. Her new baby's cries reminded her that she alone had to feed her, change her, and dress her. Chris's explanation—that they could be together if she had just given up their baby—boomeranged from her heart to her mind and back again.

This was a time in her life when she should have been finding her own voice, instead she felt as if a permanent piece of tape had been strapped across her mouth. The despair she felt could not be spoken aloud—to anyone. There were those who needed to be protected, especially Chris. The truth of her tears and poverty could only bring ruin to his standing in the church. And so, she remained silent.

Out of options, she boarded a city bus with Christa in her arms and rode around, contemplating the hopelessness of this new existence. Here she was, on welfare, living in a sketchy apartment in an even worse neighborhood. She had exactly a hundred and forty-eight dollars in government assistance to her name. Because she'd refused to allow her baby to be adopted, she'd soon be cut off financially from the Mercy League, a problem that weighed heavily on her heart. As bad as her apartment was, at least it was better than being homeless, which was bound to be her fate if she didn't get help.

She had to do something to better her situation, for Christa's sake. She felt alone in this painful journey, and alone she was guaranteed to be.

Unless she did something about it.

After riding around for hours, carefully weighing the pros and cons of the plan that had begun to form, Diane got off the bus in the Crenshaw District in south Los Angeles. Clutching the precious little baby in her arms, she finally approached the door to the apartment where her father, Joe, lived. Anywhere else in the world would be better than this, but her circumstances had left her with little choice.

She barely knocked, half hoping he wouldn't answer. But the door swung open and Joe emerged in a cloud of cigar smoke. He grinned like a big drunk bear, but one look at her turned his smile into a frown.

"What you doin' here, girl?" His gin-soaked eyes darted past her, adding to the sting of his not even calling her by name. "Come on in here." He stepped aside, chopping an angry hand through the smoke. "Somebody might think that baby's mine."

Diane took a deep breath and plunged forward. Pressing her lips to her baby's forehead, she whispered, "She's your granddaughter. Christa."

He quickly shut the door behind her, his eyes narrowing in suspicion. "Lemme see her."

Diane pulled the blanket from her infant's sleeping face, displaying Christa with pride.

"She's a White lookin' little thing, ain't she?" Joe laughed. "I'm sure yo' mama's happy about that! She don't like nothin' dark . . ." He pointed his cigar at Diane and squinted through the smoke. ". . . includin' you and me."

Diane breathed deeply, summoning her courage. Just above the deafening beat of her trembling heart, she exhaled, and out came the gist of her plan.

"Dad..." She paused, waiting to see if the term of endearment she'd shunned when he'd stopped acting like a father would soften him to her proposition. "I need some help. I wanna go to school. I could get somebody to watch her for me. I just need a better place to stay."

"Oh, hell no!" he said, without even giving the option a second's thought. "You need to go on back to yo' mama's!"

"You just admitted she's not good to me. You know I can't go back there."

"Well, you ain't stayin' here!" He was already shuffling her toward the door.

"No, just listen." Her voice trembled. If she wound up back in that hallway, there'd be nothing left but the streets. "I was hoping I could live in that property you have over on Fifth."

He shook his head. "I'm 'a rent that place out. No."

"But it's empty now." Diane reasoned.

"Gotta get that heater fixed and that window in the kitchen." Joe stepped away as if the conversation was over.

"That's cool," Diane said, following. "I could just live there until you get a tenant."

He shut his eyes. "No."

"Daddy . . ." Tears finally found their way down her face as her desperation escalated. "Don't you love me?"

"Girl, I ain't never loved nobody 'cept my brother. And he's dead."

Diane swallowed hard. She'd long suspected that the sad death of her uncle had hardened Joe's heart beyond repair. As his daughter, it was hard not to take that personally.

"Look here, lemme give you some advice." Joe pointed a jittery finger at her face. "You're young and pretty. You got a nice figure. Get you an old man wit' some money and let him pay your bills."

Diane's stomach churned and her mind raced. Her lips quivered to defend herself, but no sound came out. She struggled just to breathe.

"Hell, that's what I do, and them girls do whatever I want 'em to do! 'Cause I pay their bills."

His words bit at her like vipers, each more poisonous than the last.

Then, as if it were possible to be hollowed out yet still alive, he added, "It ain't like you're still a virgin."

Is that what a young, desperate, scared mother is to graduate to? A kept woman?

There was nothing for her there, just more darkness. Diane vowed in her heart that this would be the last time she'd ever see Joe.

She gathered her baby closer and headed for the door. As she bolted from his apartment, she practically collided with a pretty young woman wearing a tight minidress and too much lipstick.

The girl looked Diane up and down, as if marking her territory and trying to intimidate a rival. Then she sashayed up to Joe's door and fell into his embrace.

Her eyes burning from the stomach-churning mixture of cigar smoke, cheap drugstore perfume, and bitter rejection, Diane turned her back on the man who was her father.

***

With few choices remaining, Diane found herself standing at her mother's front door.

Liz threw her arms out and enthusiastically cried, "Ooo, lemme see my grandbaby!"

Diane would've enjoyed—and probably needed—a hug, but she lied to herself that seeing the happiness baby Christa brought to her mother was good enough.

Liz cradled the baby in her arms and marveled at her bright, sleeping face. "She's beautiful," she said without looking up. She pressed her lips onto Christa's forehead and touched the feather-like red hair. "Just perfectly beautiful."

"Thanks," Diane whispered, feeling as though she'd finally produced something Liz approved of. Diane dreaded the question that would likely come next; *Who is this baby's father?*

But instead of asking about the father, Liz said, "Are you still breast feeding her or bottle feeding?"

"B-bottle feeding." Diane stumbled over her reply. "I give her a little cereal, too." Diane rummaged through her purse and produced a bottle. "I-I've got everything for her. Diapers . . . even a little teething ring."

Liz squinted at her daughter. "Okay. Why you so nervous, Diane? Go on in there and get something to eat. You look a mess, girl." Liz cooed at the baby as she was waking from her nap. "You want Meme to look after you, little Christa? Yes, I will. I will." She smiled.

Diane raided her mom's refrigerator and lucked out on leftover roast from the previous evening. It tasted like home. She grabbed her plate and stood in the doorway of the kitchen just watching her mother play with Christa. By now, Liz had changed the baby's diaper, redressed her, and was feeding her a bottle while singing a made-up song of "Meme's pretty girl is her world . . ."

Looking through the lens of loneliness, Diane thought to herself, *She must know. My mom must know that my baby's father is White.* But why hadn't Liz asked for details? Was she intentionally avoiding the question, and if so, why? It wasn't like Diane knew a ton of White boys.

When is the "Who's the daddy" question going to land? Diane worried. Would it be after dinner? Once her siblings, Fern, Vicky, and Bryant, got home? *How do I ready myself for the blowup that will surely follow?* Diane became even more nervous, and the bites of food went down her throat like rocks.

She's gotta know this is Father Chris's baby, Diane told herself as she put her plate in the sink and rinsed it to the tune of Liz's lullaby.

The sweet music of Liz's song and the laughter from the next room didn't erase the fact that Diane was carrying a dangerous secret—one that could destroy so many lives.

"I don't want him hurt," she whispered to the kitchen window. "I still want us to be a family, but I can't have him. He belongs to the priesthood."

"She spit up," Liz called out. "Bring me a towel."

Wiping a stray tear from her cheek, Diane brought Liz the towel and watched her fuss over every detail of cleaning up her grandbaby with both pleasure and pride.

Meanwhile, Diane scanned the living room—a crucifix, a peaceful picture of Jesus, prayer beads . . . All this reminded her that Liz held the church as such a divine place. No way could Diane divulge the identity of her baby's father.

Surely, she'd be accused of seducing the man of God, an unforgivable sin.

Once again, despair overshadowed Diane like a thick, dark cloud, and thoughts of taking her life consumed her. *Just end it all,* the ominous voice inside of her whispered. *No one will care. Chris certainly isn't going to marry you now.*

For a brief moment, the voice of reason argued back. *Christa needs you! If you end your life, who will take care of her?*

She even considered the unthinkable—the possibility of taking Christa's life along with her own. Her mind was racked with confusion. "Make these voices stop," she whispered.

Diane overheard Christa's cooing as Liz gently rocked the baby in her arms. For the moment, Diane was able to shake off the darkness. For now, both she and her baby were safe. At home. And no longer alone.

6

LEARNING
TO SWIM

It was by the grace of God that my mother, Diane, graduated from being suicidal to being a student at Stanford University in Northern California.

When I was around three years old, the two of us moved to Palo Alto where I'd attend her college study sessions alongside her. Sometimes, I'd sit for hours in the university's library, coloring and playing the "quiet game" while my mother was neck-deep in a textbook. Education was important to Mama. I picked up on that early on. She was already preparing me for a future in which we'd both earn college degrees.

While I can't remember her advice to me at such a tender age, I imagine it was the same she repeated many times throughout my life: "Christa, never rely on anyone to take care of you. You're going to have to take care of yourself."

Whether she was teaching me to be patient while she studied, to put away my own toys without help, or to understand the value of higher education, she was trying to prepare me for a future much like the one she envisioned for herself. One in which I'd have to be brave and strong, and prepared to manage life on my own.

If there was one thing Mama and I had already learned, it was that we couldn't rely on any man to protect or to provide.

My mother's motivations were mostly personal ones—she had something to prove, both to her own mother and to Father Chris. But maybe it was more than that. Maybe she had something to prove to herself too.

I have vague but warm memories from that period of our lives. Mostly, I recall feeling loved. Now when I think of these early years, I feel close to my mother. I feel safe and secure. I also find evidence of her determination to care for her little girl, no matter how many hardships she faced.

For instance, she enrolled me in swim lessons, which I'm certain she couldn't afford. I can picture it clearly still. There I was; all excited, with a big smile, wearing my flowered swim cap and my bright pink swimsuit purchased from the secondhand store where we bought most of our clothes.

"You need to know how to swim," Mama said, always trying to teach me something new.

I couldn't have realized it then, but now I see that there in the sparkling blue waters of our apartment pool, she was teaching me a much larger lesson, a lesson about survival.

"You swim too?" I asked, wondering why she wasn't getting in the pool.

"I already know how to swim," she said, matter-of-factly. "Now go on and listen to your teacher. I'll be right here watching."

As instructed, I held my breath, plugged my nose, and plunged my face under the sunlit surface of the water. In time, I would swim the distance of the pool, a skill that would prove useful on many levels as life later brought waves of emotional turbulence and threatened to drag me to the bottom of the deep.

Looking back, I now know my mother did her best for me. For the two of us. Always. But her own pain kept her distant. While I didn't understand it as a child, I can now see she was battling back from an unhealthy emotional place with very few coping skills to help her heal and become whole again. She was doing the best she could do, despite a million obstacles in her way.

By the time I was four years of age, it was time to enroll me in preschool. With me tugging at her shirt and her arms full of textbooks, my mother pursued the local preschool director.

"Is there any way you could just charge me for two days instead of three?"

"Well, I don't know, we don't usually—"

"I'm an English major at Foothill College." Standing a little taller and with a determination in her tone, Mama explained. "I could only afford one semester at Stanford, so . . . I've had to transfer."

The preschool director softened and looked at me with a warm smile. "We'll work something out for you. Bring your little girl back tomorrow."

Thanks to this stranger's compassion and generosity, I was able to attend the preschool program while my mother continued her studies. I loved preschool! It gave me a chance to be around other children. I loved my preschool teachers too. Not to mention the animated story time, meals, songs, games, toys, and of course, nap time.

Life wasn't perfect for our little family of two, but it was good. Our basic needs were being met, and we were working toward a better day.

Then one afternoon, I was playing outside when I discovered a big surprise. I smiled all the way up the stairs to our second-floor apartment. In my four-year-old mind, the heavens had gifted me with a shiny new pink bike.

As I wrestled to get the bike into our humble apartment, my mother came from the bedroom.

"Christa, what is that?"

"A bike, Mama."

"Where did you get it?"

"I found it right outside by the pool," I said proudly.

"It's not yours, baby. You have to give it back."

"No, Mama! I found it. It's mine!"

"It's somebody else's bike."

With me in tears and following close behind, my mom wheeled the bike back to the pool area. By this time, a concerned crowd had formed around a shrieking mother and her distraught five-year-old.

Someone shouted, "There she is! She stole the bike!"

I slid behind Mama.

"Wait just a minute!" Mama defended. "My daughter didn't steal anything. She didn't know it belonged to anyone and she's bringing it back."

There she stood, in all her pride, taking my defense. On that day, she was like a superhero, and I could hide behind her protection as she reasoned with the angry neighbor.

Finally, the other mother backed down and halfheartedly thanked us for returning the bike. As we walked back to our apartment, I reached up to clasp Mama's hand and laced my fingers in hers. In that moment, she and I were close, and I was safe.

We were not alone.

***

In the absence of my father, Mama did her best to protect me. Circumstances forced her to fill all roles. This seemed to fuel her determination to finish school. She knew education was the vehicle by which she'd be able to attain a better life for us.

On the rare occasions when she wasn't working on college assignments, we'd escape via the radio. I recall listening very attentively as the announcer introduced that evening's murder mystery plot. I didn't necessarily have an appreciation for the macabre at that age, but the nightly show was an opportunity for me to spend time with Mama in her world. On some occasions, I'd get really scared on account of that evening's entertainment. Sometimes she'd let me be her little girl and snuggle with her in her twin bed, even though my own was just a few feet away.

Our little second-floor apartment was often filled with music from the radio. One of my favorites was "Rock the Boat" by the Hues Corporation. I'd dance around the living room singing my heart out. It was a tune that would spirit my mother into a fun dance session with me, forgetting the plights of the world, her studies, and our poverty. The chance to laugh a little. . . Well, what kid would pass that up?

One day, right after we'd sung my favorite part, the music suddenly stopped. It was replaced with breaking news that another young Black man had been gunned downed by the Oakland Police.

Mama turned up the volume and cried real tears in response. I wondered if she knew the man that the reporter was talking about.

In a way, she did know him. He was the umpteenth victim of this all-too-frequent inner-city occurrence. Although some forward progress had been made, the racial climate in America was still bleak if you were Black.

"Mama, why are you crying?"

While there was no way she could explain the depth of her tears to a four-year-old, these crimes against people of color struck a painful chord in my mother's heart because she too had experienced injustice and prejudice all of her life. So, along with her collegiate pursuits, she began to educate herself in other areas.

And thus began my real education.

I'm pretty certain other four-year-olds would go to bed listening to stories about Goldilocks and the Three Bears and Humpty Dumpty. My mother would tell me stories about Crispus Attucks, a Black man who was said to be the first casualty of the American Revolution.

I would come to learn about other important figures, such as Marcus Garvey, Malcom X, Fredrick Douglass, and other revolutionary thinkers. My mother fought very hard so that I wouldn't have disdain for being Black, but instead a love and unwavering appreciation for those who had dark skin, fuller lips, and kinky hair, like her. She wanted to make sure that I loved her and that I not only would know my own African American heritage but would take pride in it too.

I didn't know anything about the Swedish side of the family— my dad's side. His decision to be absent forfeited his importance. But my confusion grew as I'd compared my pale skin to Mama's dark tones.

"Christa, it doesn't matter if your skin is white and your hair is straight," my mother would explain. "If you have one drop of Black blood in you, that makes you Black. You understand?"

I nodded as if I did, although as a child I didn't understand why she was so passionate about these sorts of things. There was a fire in her eyes when she talked about our heritage and the brave people who had sacrificed, even given their lives, in pursuit of equality for all.

My mother taught me that being Black was nothing to be ashamed of. She worked hard to give me a positive self-image.

Although she didn't realize it at the time, the lens through which I'd see myself had already begun to crack at that early age. With so much focus on skin color and hair texture, deep seeds of insecurity and confusion were taking root.

My mother's growing passion for racial justice led her to enroll me in Nairobi Preschool in Palo Alto, California. Nairobi was an Afrocentric hub where I was surrounded by blackness—teachers, children, parents, activists, and community leaders filled our lives, and Black was beautiful!

Soon my mother stopped straightening her hair and began embracing a natural Afro. I remember pleading with her to please, "Make my hair look like yours, Mama."

"No, baby," she'd say, gently holding the weight of my long red ponytails in her hands. "We don't need to cut your hair."

I just wanted to fit in to the frame of my existence, and yet there was no way to fully communicate that burning desire. I asked her this same question again and again, until eventually, I broke her.

She agreed to cut my hair. Finally, my dreams of a crowning Afro fit for a little princess would be realized. I sat still on a stool in the bathroom waiting for, and cheering on, my transformation.

My mother hesitated and then, finally . . . *snip, snip*. My long, red ponytails fell to the bathroom floor.

When I took a look in the mirror, I was devastated. I sobbed uncontrollably for hours. To my shock, I didn't look like my mother at all. My hair didn't suddenly turn into an Afro just because it'd been cut short. Instead, it curled up into tight little red ringlets.

"I look like a boy!" I cried.

Of course, I didn't want to go back to school for fear of being teased by the other kids. But that didn't stop Mama from dragging me into that tiny classroom the next day, where all eyes landed on me. The transformation tanked. I think my teachers were in shock, too.

"Why did your mother cut off your beautiful ponytails?" one of them asked.

I didn't possess the words to explain.

7

A NEW RELIGION

O ur attempt to find "religion" conjures up vivid memories from my childhood. For obvious reasons, Mama had abandoned the Catholic faith. However, there was still a part of her that was in search of a holy creator—a higher power. This longing for a spiritual enlightenment led us to the Nation of Islam.

Enter into our lives: The Honorable Elijah Muhammad, the charismatic leader of those who were known as Black Muslims in the 1970s. This man was considered by some to be a prophet. They called him "The Messenger." His book, *Message to the Black Man in America*, became our new Bible.

The Messenger was fair skinned, with an unusual voice, touting to us the visions Allah had given him. I, as all the Nation's children were made to do, carried a copy of *Message to the Black Man*. Even at five years old, I protested in small ways, intentionally losing my book.

Thus, my rebellion of the Nation began quite early.

Despite my resistance, the Nation affected every aspect of my young life. My mom switched me from public school to a private school for Black Muslim children. Now, separated from the few friendships I'd made at my old school, I was plunged into a strange new academic world and forced to adapt.

Aside from the mandatory 3Rs (Reading, 'Riting, and 'Rithmetic), my Muslim school demanded that we march!

My six-year-old self, asked, "Uh . . . is this supposed to be recess?"

I must be clear here. We did not just march around as if singing the perils of poor Humpty Dumpty—something our wiggly bodies could dance and skip to until we all fell down in a bottomless giggle.

No. We marched in step, in perfect formation while cadence chanting: "Elijah Muhammad, your left! Elijah Muhammad, your right! The White man is the devil! Sound off one, two . . . three, four!"

If the White man was the devil, what did that make me? The spawn of Satan?

Each day, I'd grind my way through the school day knowing there was one bright spot waiting after dismissal—Margaret, my babysitter.

I adored Margaret. Her home was fun-loving and filled with lots of toys and her own brood of children. One of them owned a Big Wheel, which I would ride for hours. I looked forward to Margaret's warm hospitality every day after school as she offered me a safe and happy refuge, a home away from home.

But the Nation required change as well as solidarity. We had to band together. We were taught to support the businesses of our fellow Muslims. So, Mama replaced Margaret's happy home with a seventy-year-old woman's second-floor apartment. This stranger was to be my new babysitter. In complete contrast to Margaret, this new sitter kept stashes of brown throat lozenges lying around, the ones that taste like root beer. Her place was dreary, stuffy, and cloaked with the smell of medicine and mothballs.

One afternoon, when Mama was picking me up from my new babysitter's house, I overheard the woman telling Mama about a dead duck that she was keeping in her refrigerator. Hearing her talk about the duck made me so afraid. Aside from the fear of the dead duck somehow coming back to life and attacking me, I didn't like going to her house because there weren't any kids for me to play with there.

I longed for the comfort and familiarity of Margaret's home.

Until one day. The day I rebelled.

Never short on resources, the Nation had a van that took neighborhood kids to its Muslim schools, picked us up after class, and dropped us with our assigned caregivers each afternoon.

That day when my stop came up, I bounded out of the van to the second-story apartment but had already made up my mind. I raced back to the van within seconds.

"She's not home." I lied and had the driver drop me off at Margaret's house instead.

Margaret greeted me sweetly. She seemed to understand my struggle to adapt to the changes that were being thrust upon me.

I looked different in my Muslim school uniform, an outfit that resembled something from Disney's *Aladdin*. She reached to touch my hair, now covered by a scarf. It seemed obvious to her that I didn't like my new life, and the fact that I'd shown up at her door unannounced after months of no contact clearly told her the whole story.

She smiled, sent me off to play with her children, and promptly called my mom, who was not happy about having to leave work early to come and pick me up.

Later that night, I got in trouble for lying and was sent to bed early. It didn't stop me from plotting future escapes, but sadly I never saw Margaret again.

My only freedom came on those rare occasions when we'd visit Mama's sisters, Fern and Vicky, back in LA. Around my aunts, I could take a break from the 3Rs of the Nation—Rules, Regulations, and Restrictions—and just be a little girl again.

The Nation bore so many "couldn'ts." Women couldn't be out after dark. We couldn't eat pork or pork-based foods, or Ritz Crackers and Oreo Cookies. Women couldn't show bare skin and had to be clothed in loose garments. We couldn't let even a day pass without praying three times!

I was desperate to escape, and escape I could when I was with my beloved aunts.

"I don't know why yo' mama got you wearin' this scarf!" Aunt Vicky would complain, as she'd remove it to reveal my curls.

My beautiful red hair had always brought me positive attention from adults, and my Aunt Vicky was no exception. She would lovingly take her time brushing my long red locks, reminding me how lucky I was to have this "good hair."

Aunt Vicky was also a disciplinarian. In her opinion, there was a definite divide between *grown folks* and children. I was often scolded for crossing that boundary.

"A child should stay in a child's place," she would say. Although she was well aware of the reasoning behind my not knowing the proper adult-child etiquette. "Yo' mama needs to let you be a child! Go put some regular clothes on!" She would shout these assertions in a way that read my thoughts exactly. With her insistence, I'd race out to play, looking like my cousins and the rest of the kids.

Freedom!

For those precious weekends at Aunt Vicky's house, I could ditch the round Aladdin hat with a star and crescent moon on the front, the Ali Baba pants with elastic at the ankle, and the double-breasted jacket with Nehru collar. A borrowed pair of Toughskin jeans and a faded unicorn T-shirt from my cousins was all I needed to fit in.

Visits to my Aunt Fern's house were an equal joy and break from the Nation. During one of those family gatherings, someone carved a beautiful ham in the kitchen and slid me a warm piece of the forbidden pork and whispered, "Here, your mom won't know."

It was heaven in my mouth.

Needless to say, my aunts unwittingly played a huge role in my rebellion. My young mind wondered how something so delicious could be so wrong. I thought the same thing about bacon, Ritz Crackers, and Oreo Cookies. I questioned it all.

Of course, the Nation wasn't all bad.

Its appeal to Blacks was that the Nation taught us self-respect. It was there that we learned a history that was different from the history we'd been taught in school. Through the lessons of the Nation, I learned that black skin signified royalty. We were descendants of kings and queens, intelligent people, not savages. They taught us that King Solomon, one of the wisest men to have ever lived, was Black.

The Nation taught its members to abandon the moniker of slavery's surnames like Johnson, Smith, and Brown. Hence, the late Malcom Little, the ex-con and street hustler, had reinvented himself as Malcom X, the outspoken, iconic, and prolific lieutenant of the Nation.

The "prophet" Elijah Muhammad challenged us to ditch societal vices of drugs, alcohol, and crime. Equality could only be had when we as a people pursued education, owned our own businesses, took care of our minds and bodies, respected ourselves, and became exemplary citizens.

Elijah Muhammad's teachings drew my mother in. Perhaps finally now she could be loved and respected, not despite her blackness, but because of it. The Nation taught Black men to celebrate the beauty of Black women and their families. Women in the Nation adorned themselves in modesty and exuded a natural beauty that came from within.

The identity transformation wasn't complete in the Nation without a name change. So, my mother became Diane 12X.

Blacks like my mother were also admonished to abandon Christianity because it was the religion that had been used by White slave owners to keep their slaves compliant.

Elijah Muhammad's contemporary, Dr. Martin Luther King, Jr., was criticized by Muslims and other groups, like the Black Panthers, because of his nonviolent stance. Turning the other cheek, peaceful protests, and breaking Jim Crow laws was no way to gain equal footing, according to the Nation's leaders. We had been submissive and patient long enough, and it hadn't gotten us anywhere.

Some who were disenfranchised because of the injustice and inequalities of the day were persuaded to join the Nation of Islam and adopt its militaristic teachings as a way of life. And my mother was *all in*.

***

It wasn't long after joining the Nation that Mama would have an arranged marriage to Norman from Alabama. Norman was quickly moving up the ranks in the Nation by following orders from the men in charge.

He had grown up in the South and had personally endured the brutal abuses of the Jim Crow culture. Billie Holiday's lament of "Strange Fruit"—a song about dead Black men hanging prominently from trees—was something Norman knew firsthand, and it had fueled his trek to California, where he hoped to escape an uncertain fate.

The regimented practices of the Nation were just the thing to make one twenty-five-year-old southern Black man feel empowered by an army of thousands. But is there room in the heart for a wife and kids when it's already filled with anger and rage? That was a question the Nation could not answer.

Diane was still very tender and reeling from the pain of the broken promises made by Father Chris and the Catholic church. *The Message to the Black Man* and the Nation offered her a new salvation.

Norman did his best with the instant family he'd been tasked with. He adopted me and gave me his last name, something my own father had never done. Norman's kind act was a step toward repairing my wound of abandonment. He made me feel wanted and tried to fill the hole that had been so big in our lives.

Gaining momentum in the Nation now, our young and attractive little family was favored. But imagine two broken people thrust together to resemble something ideal. The pressure of being arranged must have been excruciating for Norman and Diane. Then, in the midst of all this, my brother, Hasan, was born.

Oh, how I loved being the big sister and having a baby brother of my own. I was proud to help my mom give him a bottle and change his diapers. Hasan brought tremendous joy to our family, and he gave me a constant playmate.

But his birth also regurgitated some old feelings of desertion, betrayal, and loss. Raising me by herself had been hard enough, but what if Mama had to raise both me and my brother alone? The fears my mother faced must have felt overwhelming at times, and it surely took some very deep faith to put her trust in the institution of marriage and the promises of another man after having been burned so deeply the first time.

While the Nation forged the common bond between them, they were from two different worlds. Mama was not the subservient little woman for which the Nation's gentler sex was known. Perish the thought! She was a college-educated, tough, outspoken force to be reckoned with. A true survivor who had no intention of ever again surrendering her soul for a man.

Whether preached or implied, it was understood that a husband's duty was to rule his world. The power imbalance was evident, and our little apartment eventually became a battle zone complete with shouting, crying, and slammed doors echoing throughout.

Still, Mama tried her best to fit the role she was supposed to embrace. Day after day, I'd hold my little brother and watch her in the mirror as she readied herself for temple. On went her scarf to cover her beautiful tuft of hair. I'd sit next to her white temple gown, lying starched across the bed, and in time I'd come to learn some things about my mother. You can't hide a broken heart. It's always revealed in the eyes.

Family photos of her unhappy face served as further proof that she and Norman's marriage was not the stuff of which dreams are made. For the first two years of Hasan's little life, there were heart-stopping ups and downs. I'm so glad he can't possibly remember them. The missing component of Mama and Norman's arranged union was love—both were trying to fulfill their duty to the Nation, but you can't force a connection no matter how hard you try. I rarely saw her smile. I never saw them hold hands. Theirs was not that kind of loving, romantic relationship we all imagine two beautiful people taking full advantage of.

Mama had her wounds. Norman had his own. Together, they both struggled to heal, and instead began to spiral deeper into pain.

One day, Mama went to meet with the temple elders. As was the policy and custom, the Nation's couples had to get approval for a divorce. I'm told she poured her heart out to them. Through her tears, she confessed her deepest secrets, laying bare her fears for the future of their loveless marriage.

But the elders were not going for it. Diane and Norman had been placed together by the Nation, and they were to stay together. No other option existed. So, they simply did what the Nation told them to do. We all went to temple. We all played the part. And we all felt the tensions building by the day—like screeching tires that you know will end in a life-changing impact. We just had to brace for that impact.

One night, while Norman had gone back to Alabama to visit his relatives, I watched my mother perform her beauty ritual of steaming her face. Underneath the cloak of the towel, I could hear her heaving.

I put my hand on her back and asked, "Mama, are you all right?"

Bent from nausea, she heaved again. "I'll be all right, baby."

Surely, she already knew what I would learn a few months later. She was pregnant. She and Norman had reached no real reconciliation. There had been no release of the marital tension. She was just pregnant—again—and swelling with an overwhelming fear of the future.

***

I imagine Norman felt that she needed a break when he decided to drive Hasan and me cross-country from California to Alabama. We stopped at a little motel in Phoenix, Arizona, and ate Kentucky Fried Chicken. Probably missing Mama, Hasan cried most of the trip. I missed her too, but I didn't cry. I was too busy enjoying having a father. And I was determined to make the most of this road trip that would take me far away from the Nation and the tensions of home.

Alabama was full of friendly faces and warm hearts. At the family farm, I met my new grandma—Grandmother Amelia.

"Baby, you can call me Grandma Millie," she said with a generous hug.

We were instant family. I also met my Aunt Jeanette. Jeanette, Norman's sister, was wheelchair-bound from an accident, but she offered nothing but love and kisses for Hasan and I.

Alabama couldn't have been more different from Los Angeles. Oh, that smell of homemade pancakes and biscuits in the morning was like heaven rolled into one month of forever! Those summer days were bright and swelteringly hot, but I enjoyed spending time with Norman's family and experiencing many things for the first time, like riding horses!

Accompanied by a bevy of barefoot cousins, I'd walk to the corner store for ice cream each day. We played with hogs, June bugs, roosters, and chickens (until their necks were rung in preparation for dinner). Norman's family loved on me and made me feel like I was blood. I soaked it all in.

Norman had opened a restaurant in Selma, Alabama, and had gained a reputation for making all beef burgers to order and really good bean pies. It was no small feat to get people to switch from eating sweet potato pies to bean pies. I think Norman was probably the only Black Muslim in the entire town. Everyone else was Christian (or at least, they were churchgoers).

A jukebox stood in the back of Norman's burger shack, and I loved going there to play Gladys Knight's "Midnight Train to Georgia." I spent that entire summer traipsing around those safe southern spaces, running barefooted without a care in the world.

Our lovely southern vacation had almost tricked me into believing that things in our family were good, but as soon as we all returned home to Los Angeles, the scary chaos of reality resumed.

Some months later, on February 20, my little sister, Aisha, was born.

I vividly recall the moment when I first heard the soulful voice of Stevie Wonder on the radio, singing her song, "Isn't She Lovely." The song celebrated the beauty of a baby girl named Aisha and how she was made from love. I always thought that my sister was the luckiest baby because she had a song written about her. It wasn't until years later that I discovered the truth—that Wonder had written the song for his own daughter Aisha. Despite this revelation, the song still brings a smile to my face.

Together, Diane and Norman had given life to two beautiful children. But these births couldn't make the relationship between them better. This time, when Norman returned to LA, he maintained residency at a seedy little motel on La Brea near Washington. Their issues persisted.

My having a father would be short lived.

One afternoon, Mama was having a very hard day. She'd been worrying about the bill collectors and fighting tears of frustration—there were now three mouths to feed. At her end, she put us all into the car and drove us to the raggedy little motel where Norman had been living. She put the emergency brake on and looked at each of us. Aisha was sleeping soundly. Hasan was sitting in his car seat playing with his toy.

"Okay, Christa," she said, undoing her seatbelt and looking around the parking lot. "You stay here in the car and look after your brother and sister."

Norman threw the motel room door open.

"I'll be right back," Mama said with a long exhale.

Then they both disappeared into the blackened room.

Through the open car window, I could hear their voices grow loud and angry.

"We have three kids, Norman. I'm working every day! I can't do this all on my own. You need to get a job and help me."

"I got a job, Diane! I got my own business. Just give it a little time. It'll pay off."

"A real job, Norman! Selling bean pies in Alabama ain't helpin' us right now. The Nation has done nothing for us! Nothing! I've had to go on welfare just to make ends meet."

"Wait, you collectin' welfare *and* workin'? That's fraud, Diane. You gonna fool around and end up in jail. Then what's gonna happen to the kids?"

"Well, what am I supposed to do? What's the answer?! I need help, Norman."

The next thing I heard was my mother screaming, "Christa! Christa! Get the attendant!"

They were fighting for real this time. My eyes got big, and I froze. Hasan started to cry.

After that, all my eight-year-old mind remembers is Norman's hands reaching into the car to swoop up Hasan and Aisha. My mom was crying and kissing their faces as Norman pulled them away from her.

"Mommy loves you, baby. Shh, shhh." She cried, trying to keep everyone calm. "It's gonna be okay . . ."

My mom turned to me and, as if to convince herself, repeated, "Norman's just gonna keep them for a little while, Christa. Just a little while."

She sat behind the wheel of the car for a time with her eyes closed but keeping them locked tight didn't dam her tears.

We finally drove away from the motel in silence. My mom didn't have the courage to look back, but I did. I looked out that back window until the little motel and Norman, his arms full of his babies, got swallowed up in my *never-speak-of-it-again*.

And then, they were gone.

8

NOW THAT
YOU'RE GONE

I wanted to hold on to the memory of Norman, Hasan, and Aisha but I had no choice but to tuck them away. The sudden loss of my brother, baby sister, and Norman was too much to explain. We'd gone from being a family of five to just the two of us again. And the pain was intense. Far too much to process on my own, and it seemed it was too much for Mama too. She and I never really spoke of them after that day at the motel. Looking back, I'm sure she was trying to protect me, as well as herself, from the loss of all losses. In order to survive, we had to pretend to forget. I knew my beloved siblings were somewhere out there, but where? I vowed in my heart that one day I would find them. And we would be a family once again.

During this time, Mama and I also made a slow descent from the Nation, which I was happy about. Fighting severe depression, my mom leaned on her sisters to help take care of me when she had what my family and I called "spells of darkness." Her growing instability was understandable, given the fact that she'd had so many losses in her life: her mother's sudden passing from cancer meant they'd never be able to repair their broken relationship; Father Chris had all but vanished; and now two of her children were gone.

Although my aunts had their fair share of responsibilities and financial troubles, it didn't stop them from taking me in. I'd live with them during the week and Mama would try to come get me on the weekends when she was able to. Sometimes her spells would last for several months, and I wouldn't see her at all.

I adjusted well to my new life with my aunts and cousins, Nikki, Gary, and Lisa. The four of us bonded closely and fought like real siblings do. We'd argue over who'd wash the dishes or take out the trash. We'd even fight about who'd get to sit in the front seat.

"I called shotgun," the younger ones would usually protest.

I'd always pull rank, even though I was just a few years older. I felt like I was one of the grown-ups, an old soul who'd been navigating the grown-up world since I was born.

In the 'hood, you get used to a different kind of normal. In the suburbs, moms pack lunches for their children, load them into the family van, and navigate the school carpool lines. Parents know the teachers and school administrators, some even by their first names. But it was different for those of us who grew up in the inner city of Los Angeles.

While my aunts would pack us great lunches, they had to work long hours just to make ends meet, so they had to teach us to be self-sufficient from a very young age. Just across the street from our apartment sat an elementary school, but like many public schools in underserved neighborhoods, it was underfunded and under-resourced. My aunts were forced to look elsewhere for better opportunities for us. When they discovered a school across town that would provide a safer, more enriching environment, off we went.

Angeles Mesa was in a slightly better neighborhood of Los Angeles. It would require us to take two buses to get there. On the first day of school, my Aunt Vicky rode the bus with us all the way to the school, modeling exactly how to do it.

"Get on the bus, drop in the right amount of money for the three of you, sit up front, stay together, and we'll see you when you get home."

After that first day, our seven-, eight-, and nine-year-old selves were expected to make the journey on our own. My cousin Nikki was fortunate enough to go to private school. Although her parents had been divorced for several years, her father was still very active in her life. He made sure she didn't have to be shuffled around the city, taking public transportation to school.

Meanwhile, my cousins, Gary, Lisa, and I would wake up early in the morning, dress ourselves, and head for the bus stop. To amuse myself, I invented a silly name for the RTD (Regional Transit Department). Renaming the system to Richard T. Davis somehow made me feel safer.

"Come on, guys! Hurry up!" I'd say each morning. "We don't want Uncle Richard to leave us. We can't be late again."

We'd already been called to the offices several times due to our tardiness.

As the eldest of the cousins, it was my duty to make sure we all made it to school safely. Every day, we'd ride with "Uncle Richard" from Adams Boulevard to Western Avenue. Once we got off the bus, we'd walk several long blocks to get to the school.

By the time I was in the fourth grade, my younger cousins and I had learned to navigate the public bus system like seasoned county workers. Sometimes I'd even pretend I was going to a job instead of school. I'd imagine that I was the beautiful lady who sat across from us each morning, always in the same exact spot. She smelled pretty and wore a business suit and carried a black attaché case. In my fantasy, she was married and had children. Each night when she got home from work, she was greeted at the door by her children with a barrage of kisses and hugs. Her husband was tall, dark, and handsome, and they were obviously still in love.

One day, I was deep in the fantasy when I was snapped back to reality by our bus driver.

"Young lady, don't you and your crew get off here?"

My cousins and I quickly grabbed our *Happy Days* lunch boxes—mine had an image of the Fonz on it—and exited the bus, thanking the driver for watching out for us. I loved the Fonz's character. He was street smart, and nobody messed with him. Perhaps my Fonzie lunch box would be a pseudo good luck charm, protecting us from the dangers of our neighborhood.

For several years I bounced back and forth between living with Mama or with relatives.

On one of those occasions, I was sent to live with my great-aunt. Aunt Kate was Mama's father's sister. Her mission was to somehow make restitution for her brother's failings as a father. These moves were always meant to be temporary. One never wants to "wear out their welcome." The move to Aunt Kate's house, though short lived, lasted way too long for me. To be honest, one week at her house was too long.

I dreaded staying with my mama's older, more stoic aunt. She had four boys, two of whom still lived at home. Aunt Kate wasn't used to raising girls, and I was definitely not accustomed to living with teenage boys or being treated like one.

With no man present in their lives, she did her best to run a tight ship. My cousin Pat and his brother Dell were several years older.

To describe them as mischievous teens would be an understatement. Aunt Kate laid down the law.

Like a commanding officer leading a platoon, we would be awakened each morning by a bugle horn—her voice.

"Rise and shine. It's time to get the day started."

It didn't seem to matter to her that the sun wasn't even awake at that god-forsaken hour.

"Make sure your shoes are shined and your clothes are properly ironed, Privates," she'd bark.

"There will be no eating in this house except for at the designated mealtimes; zero eight hundred hours, twelve hundred hours, and eighteen hundred hours"—yes, it was run like a military mess hall. She put a padlock on the freezer, hoping it would deter the teenage boys with voracious appetites from cleaning out the fridge. But the pair always found ways to outsmart the system.

Her rules didn't keep them from going rogue; they still managed to get into the food stash. Neither did it prevent them from pranking and terrorizing me. I dreaded being left alone with them, but there was no one to tell.

During my junior high school years, my mother settled down for a little while in a place I loved. My aunts lived right up the street from us, so they could keep a watchful eye on me if my mother's mental stability grew erratic. When she was having good days, all was well. She was fun and kind and a good mother. For a fleeting moment, my mother would let her guard down and let me into her world.

Her down days were another story. I never knew what to expect on the days that something or someone was troubling her. When she was having a challenging day, it was easier to run for the hills. And run I did, right up the street to my aunts' apartment. There I could pretend that all was normal in my world. There was a silent agreement. They didn't ask why I was there, and I didn't divulge what was going on down the street.

Growing up in "The Jungle" *which was* a low-income housing neighborhood of Los Angeles that rests west of Crenshaw to La Brea—was every bit of the experience implied in the name, but the street I grew up on was a few short blocks below the Baldwin Hills community, where wealthy Black families lived. Being in such close proximity to affluence made us somehow feel a little less poor. *Perhaps one day we might graduate from the struggle of poverty like those who live above us up the hill.*

In The Jungle, you constantly had to be on the lookout for danger because you never knew when you might encounter a predator. Very few of its residents were able to escape the dense, seemingly impenetrable, walls of The Jungle, nor its drug-induced vices. Crack cocaine was on the rise and, for some, dealing drugs became a quick means to finally having their fair share in life.

Everyone had to be careful. It didn't matter if you were a kid or an adult; trouble didn't discriminate. It was imperative to know how to take care of yourself if you were going to survive that kind of environment. The streets became even more treacherous under the cloak of darkness. I'm sure that's why we had to be home before the street lights came on. It simply wasn't safe to be outside after dark.

In The Jungle, children see and experience things long before they should. One morning, I was snatched into consciousness by the screams of a man pleading for his life.

"Help me, please someone! Help!"

I peered out of the tiny bathroom window of our apartment to get a glimpse of what was going on. I wish I could say that what I saw shocked me. Oh, I was scared, but I wasn't shocked.

The cries for help were coming from a man who was being repeatedly stabbed by another man. From my window, I saw people passing by, ignoring the man's cries. Each passerby acted as if they didn't even see the man being brutalized. They just continued walking to the other side of the street.

I don't believe they passed by because they didn't care, but because of fear. Fear of retaliation. Fear of endangering their own families. Fear that no emergency services would show up to assist them if they needed it.

Finally, an ambulance did arrive, and the victim was shuttled away. I never found out if he lived or died. I don't even remember talking about the incident with anyone. Even as a child, I'd come to expect violence in neighborhoods like mine. And I'd learned that silence was a tool for survival.

Like a chameleon, I tried various methods to camouflage myself. If I could blend in with the environment and remain inconspicuous, maybe then I would be safe. Maybe then the predators wouldn't find me. But darn my fair skin, freckled face, and flaming long red hair!

"What are you?" some snarling girl would ask me.

"What do you mean?" At first, I didn't really understand the question.

"Well, you're not Black!"

I didn't really know how to answer that question. I only saw myself as Black. If I wasn't Black and I wasn't White. What was I?

The fact that I was always tall for my age also made me a target. I was taller than most of the boys in my class and I had also begun to develop beyond the other girls my age. This brought unwanted attention not only from the hormonal boys in my neighborhood, but also from older men. These men were often intoxicated, and hung out near the liquor store, which we kids would frequent to buy candy and Hostess cupcakes. They would proposition young girls like me at a very early age.

My life in The Jungle was akin to that of Little Red Riding Hood. All she wanted to do was to make it to Grandma's house. Unfortunately, the woods weren't a safe place for Red Riding Hood. Unbeknownst to her, there was a wolf lurking in the woods who had evil intentions toward her. The wolves in my neighborhood would try to hide themselves under the cloak of darkness. Thankfully, I knew better than to get caught in a trap. I'd run away as fast as I could.

The Jungle life was constantly robbing us of our innocence. One summer day, some friends and I were waiting at a bus stop, anticipating a splashing good time at the local swimming pool. A man pulled up in a car and tried to get our attention, but we were kind of oblivious. He kept talking to us from his driver's window, trying to get one of us to come over to the car. We were smart enough not to comply.

It took a few minutes, but finally we realized what the man was doing, although at the time we were too young to know the term for it. The man was exposing himself to us from behind the wheel of his car. He eventually sped off, and we went on about our day. But you never get images like that out of your head.

For some strange reason, I never felt safe enough to tell anyone about these incidents. For me, there was an inner knowing that I didn't have anyone to protect me. No big brothers, no uncles, and no father to come to my rescue. No one to chase off the dangers of The Jungle. I learned early in life that if I were to survive, I would need to be self reliant. I was it!

Not only did my physical appearance make me prey to men, but it also made me the prey of mean girls. They seemed to hate me because of how I looked. My fair skin and straight hair made me a target in my own neighborhood, in the very place where I was supposed to belong.

Colorism was the ugly after effect of slavery. Slaves who worked in the house, and who had fair skin, often enjoyed privileges that those who worked in the fields were not afforded. Having more European features meant that you were better. And unfortunately, that hadn't changed even though we were living in the 20th Century.

I now understand that the girls who bullied me did so because they hated their own dark skin. They were made to loathe their own natural and God-given beauty. But the truth was that those girls and I were more alike than they knew. I could relate to their feelings of inadequacy and rejection. I too was wrestling with those same feelings.

"You think you're cute, don't you?" one of them would fire at me.

Before I could deny it, another would shout out, "You think you're better than us because you have long, good hair, huh? Well, you ain't better than us."

I'll never forget the day I was cornered and outnumbered by eight of them in our apartment corridor. One of the girls was an old classmate of mine. I tried to smile at her, hoping to win her over. I'd always tried really hard to stay to myself in school, to lay low and steer clear of any trouble. I didn't even really talk to the other kids; I was too afraid.

But the girls were rallying each other now, growing more vicious as they circled around me. *I think I'm cute?? Seriously? I'm the ugliest girl I know. I hate my red hair and fair skin. I've even vowed to dye my hair black as soon as I'm old enough.* But how do you explain that you hate what you see in the mirror just as much as they do?

I was so afraid, that I was sure I was going to throw up, or worse, wet my pants right there in front of them. I was much taller than most of them, which meant that I probably could have taken out a few of them, but I was a *scaredy cat.*

The most intimidating of the girls, a known female gang member, struck first by pushing me from behind.

"What you gonna do about it?" Another girl got so close to me that I could feel her hot breath on me. "We should cut that pretty face!"

What am I going to do about it? I began to scan my surroundings in hopes of coming up with some sort of an emergency exit strategy.

I'm terrified! I don't want them to cut my face. God, help me!

By nothing less than a miracle, a friend appeared out of nowhere. "What up, Christa?"

I felt frozen, like I was trapped in a nightmare; the kind where you keep trying to speak but can't.

When I was finally able to answer, my voiced cracked. "What's up with you, Sean?"

Normally, I despised Sean; he was annoying. But that day, he was a godsend.

He distracted the girls just long enough to grant me a small opening in the circle. Taking advantage of the moment, I began walking away, almost in slow motion. I just needed to make it to my apartment, which was mere steps in front of me. My legs felt heavy, like I'd run a full marathon, but I didn't dare look back at the angry mob. It felt like one of those recurring nightmares. The ones in which you're yelling as loud as you possibly can but no one can hear you. Your cries go unanswered.

As I made it to my front door, my hands were shaking so much that I could barely get the key in the door. When I finally got inside our empty apartment, I bolted the door behind me. My heart was still racing when I grabbed some food from the kitchen, turned on the TV, and tried to forget that afternoon's events.

The next morning at school, I met up with my friend Carol. As we stood in line to get breakfast and hot chocolate, I told her about almost being jumped the day before. My heart began to race all over again, as if I'd been transported back to the scene of the incident. Carol suddenly looked afraid herself.

"What's the matter?" I asked.

She grabbed my arm and said, "Don't look now but there's a girl standing behind you, looking at you crazy. Is that her?"

I was too afraid to turn around and look. When I finally summoned the courage, I was mortified! It was her. She didn't go to my school. *How had she found me?*

"I gotta go!" I left my friend Carol standing in the cafeteria line.

Under normal circumstances, I avoided the office at all costs, but that day I welcomed it as a sanctuary.

The school secretary peered at me over her glasses. "Why aren't you in class?"

"I have an urgent, private matter to discuss with my counselor," I said, hoping she wouldn't pry any further. The last thing I wanted was to be labeled a *snitch!*

A few minutes later, I sat in my counselor's office, explaining my plight in one big run-on sentence. Showing compassion, she pulled the yellow early-dismissal slip from her desk drawer, wrote my name on it, and told me she was sending me home.

"Who should I call to talk to about this matter?" she asked.

I wished I could have told her to call my father or Mama, that they'd take care of this. But I knew better. Mama was always working, my stepfather Norman was gone, and my real father . . . well, he had chosen never to be in the picture at all.

That day I would have made my PE teacher proud. I finally ran the mile in under seven minutes flat, a feat I hadn't been able to accomplish all semester. It's amazing how fear can empower you, if you don't let it crush you first.

The counselor did follow up with my mom at work that afternoon, explaining what had happened and making sure I had made it home safely. The next day, Mama withdrew me from that school. I never saw Carol again. While that particular group of girls wouldn't be able to harm me, I'd face many other dangerous situations over the next several years, all of which I would narrowly escape.

9

CRIMINAL
ACTIVITY

In a strange twist of fate, the traumatic encounter with the violent gang presented me with a new opportunity. I got the chance to switch schools. The best part was that this time we didn't have to resort to our usual tactics— I didn't have to lie about where I lived or use someone else's address. Because of the bullying, my transfer was immediately approved by the school district. I was entering a whole new world.

John Burroughs Jr. High School was located in a much nicer, more affluent, mostly Jewish neighborhood. The people there ate lox and bagels, and men wore long beards and odd black suits. Before transferring to JB, I'd never even heard of lox or bagels. My neighborhood corner store sold Hostess Twinkies and pickled pigs' feet! There was nothing Kosher about my community.

Although JB was nestled in a mostly Jewish community, it was diverse. JB attracted students from all over LA. I didn't dare ask how they had gotten there. I was just happy to feel safe. The kids were more accepting at JB. They didn't seem to notice that I was different. And although my feelings of being an outsider never fully went away, I began to forge new friendships.

A friend from my neighborhood also transferred to JB with me. I'm not sure how her parents had gotten her into the school. She'd been sworn to secrecy.

"My mom said that we can't tell anyone where you and I really live." We made a pact that day, which we both kept until today.

Initially, Cheryl and I heavily relied on one another for emotional support. It was helpful to have a familiar friend in my new environment. We went from being girls from the wrong side of the tracks to "normal girls." Of course, normal has a price.

As it is with any school, the cool kids usually determine what's fashionable for all the rest of us who are trying to fit in. Cheryl and I were certain that owning a pair of Gloria Vanderbilt jeans, an Izod shirt, and white K-Swiss tennis shoes would assure our entrance into the "cool kids' club." There was only one small problem—my body was definitely not built for Gloria Vanderbilt jeans, but I didn't let that deter me from squeezing my chubby figure into them anyway. My curves at the time seemed to be in all the wrong places. I had misplaced "cushion" on the front side that I wished I could move to my backside. I envied the girls my age who had waistlines and hips. I still do, I must confess.

As Cheryl and I began to expand and make new relationships, our friendship eventually drifted apart. But I'll always be grateful for her. She helped to make the transition to a new school easier for me and made me feel less alone.

Enter into my world—Maya Angelou. Of course, she wasn't the real Maya Angelou. I called her that because she had a flair for the dramatic.

One day, as I was sitting in my fourth period English class, in walks this unusually bubbly girl. I found her to be a little odd. She carried a huge ledger with her, the kind they might have used in the 1950s to do bookkeeping.

"Hi, I'm Valorie Day," she said. "I'm a writer."

Okay, I thought to myself, *you are taking yourself waaaaay too seriously.* After all, we were only in middle school!

Valorie was different. Even the way she introduced herself boasted of her self-confidence. She would always articulate her name in a long, drawn-out manner, as if to say, *I'm going to be famous someday. You all just don't know it yet!*

I was in the presence of a real-life author, according to her. I tried to ignore the chance encounter between the prolific novelist and myself. I definitely didn't want to end up as one of the characters in the novel she was working on during class! And besides, we didn't really have anything in common; my passion was for singing, not writing.

As far back as I could remember, music called to me. I would spend hours listening to my aunts' records. I loved Natalie Cole, Roberta Flack, and Phyllis Hyman, but I felt a special connection to Teena Marie. Her soulful R&B songs lamented of being different, something I could relate to. She was a White woman who had been raised in a predominately African American neighborhood, in Los Angeles. We were kindred spirits—what came out of our mouths challenged what people saw on the outside.

I would pore over her songs, mimicking every note and bend. Of course, the lyrics were way too mature for my life experience. I felt free when I sang. Music was a place of solace for me— a place where I could escape. I could be someone else. Singing also brought me some much-needed affirmation.

"You can sing, girl," people would say, and I liked that.

As a young girl, I dreamed of taking my talents on *The Gong Show*—the *American Idol* of my day. I loved singing. Pop, jazz, R&B . . . it didn't matter what it was as long as it had soul.

After school one day, I overheard a girl asking Valorie and her friend Collette what they were going to do for the school talent show.

"We're going to sing 'A Taste of Honey' by Sukiyaki," said Valorie, referring to the popular chart topper in 1981.

Wait, what? I stopped to listen as they sang a few lines. Their harmonies were beautiful and drew me in. I couldn't believe it; Valorie could sing! From then on, I knew we'd be friends.

Being friends with Valorie—who, by the way, insisted on being called by her full name and not *Val*—meant that I'd be involved in her fictional worlds. Although I didn't like it, I eventually became one of the characters in her ninth-grade novel. *The Furious Five* was a story about the misadventures of five high school girlfriends. She even made pop-up paper puppets in our likenesses. How could I go wrong with a friend who followed her creative whims to fruition or failure?

The first time I spent the night at her house was an unusual weekend for me. Her mother was home, and she cooked a big meal for us. The next morning, we awoke to the most delectable smell — fresh baked biscuits, scrambled eggs, bacon, grits, juice, and all the fixins.

" Uh, is this a special occasion?" I asked.

Valorie squinted at me and smiled. "Girl, what do you mean? It's just Saturday morning breakfast like my mom always makes. What's the big deal?"

I played along. "No big deal," I said, for fear of being embarrassed about my own home life.

That morning, we sat around the table with her mom and her sister, Stacy. I studied them as they laughed and talked over breakfast. Valorie's Scottish terrier, Charlie, licked my feet beneath the dining table. I guessed it was to get my attention, so I snuck him a few scraps. It seemed the thing to do on that Saturday of things I'd never done before.

Mama Shirley, as I called her, asked me questions about my family and about how Valorie and I had met one another. I'd practiced an alternative version of my life so many times that it was easy for me to hide the heavy stuff from most people. My life was full of secrets, and I was especially good at keeping them.

I felt instantly loved by Mama Shirley. She had a very comforting way about her.

Later that day, we went window shopping at Ohrbach's Department Store. In our case, window shopping was code for *You may not ever get the outfits you're looking at unless they go on sale, or you might have to wait for back-to-school shopping time* (which was only once a year).

Much to my surprise, Valorie didn't buy anything either. That was how I discovered that Valorie and I did have some things in common—our mothers were both single moms who were barely scraping by. In Valorie's home, money may have been a little scarce but there was an abundance of love. In mine, both money and togetherness were on a slow drip.

In the ensuing years, I'd spend a lot of time at Valorie's house. Her family became my surrogate family. They took me in as one of their own. I learned quickly that Mama Shirley didn't play. She had rules in her home, and she wasn't afraid to lay down the law. One of them was that you had to make your whereabouts known.

At my house, I could pretty much come and go as I pleased. I had a lot of freedom. It was a different story at Valorie's house. A lesson I learned the hard way.

"Guess what I have?" Valorie said one day, waving an envelope in the air while wearing a devilish grin. "An *invitation*." She sang the word with a heavy dose of drama.

"To a party?" I asked, excitedly trying to see what she was holding.

"Not just a party. *The* party!" She cheered.

And she was right. The invitation wasn't just to any old party. It was *the party of the season*, hosted by the most popular girl at school and promising to have no parental supervision!

Plus . . . the coolest high school guys would surely be in attendance.

Valorie and I devised a plan. She would spend the entire weekend at my house, where the rules were lax.

I'm sure you can see where this is going. Like most teenagers, we were in hot pursuit of the edge—the edge of reason, the edge of trouble. I'd spent many weekends at Valorie's house, but this would be the first time she was staying the night at my place after having finally met my mother. Mama Shirley must've asked us fifty questions, but there was one in particular that Valorie and I tried our best to avoid:

"What time will your mother be home, Christa?"

Valorie quickly lied. "She'll be home after she gets off work, Mom. Don't worry."

I looked away so Mama Shirley wouldn't detect that we were lying. Truth was, I didn't have any idea when my mother would be home, but I could be certain it would be late.

***

"Sit still, Christa."

Valorie's nerves were piquing while she did my makeup and hair. With her creative side, I wasn't sure if I was going to end up looking good or like a complete mess. Before I knew it, she had a comb in one hand and all of my hair in the other.

"I saw this in one of Sade's music videos. It's gonna look beautiful on you!"

The singer Sade and I were kindred spirits. Her father was Nigerian, and her mother was English. I admired her sultry sound and sophisticated vibe. She was stunning!

On that night, Valorie was doing her best to recreate that same sleek ponytail look on me.

Protesting would have done me no good. Valorie was going to fulfill her glamorous vision because she was just that type—the kind of person who dabbles in fantasies.

Okay, my makeup was a little runway-ish. But the new hairstyle did make me seem more mature. The look was a perfect complement to the outfit we had stolen . . . er-uh, I mean . . . *borrowed* from her big sister, Stacy's, closet. Stacy was a few years older. She worked for a department store and had a closet full of nice things that we would sometimes use and return without her knowledge. She would never have let us wear her clothes to a party of all places, but that night we were willing to take the risk.

With our alibi perfectly in place, our hair and makeup a little *too* done, and our *stolen* clothes building our confidence, off to the party we went.

Needless to say, I felt a little anxious all night, not just because I worried about our lie but because I was terrified I'd spill something on Stacy's shirt. Valorie had far fewer fears than I did, and she instantly became the life of the party.

"You look so pretty, Christa," she said, smoothing my hair up again in our fight to defy gravity. "Bet you meet a cute boy." She reassured me, trying to get me to follow her lead.

"Yeah, right," I said. I felt like Cinderella at the ball. If it was my destiny to meet a cute guy that night, it needed to happen before the clock struck midnight.

I rarely caught the attention of the boys my age, and I usually ended up with guys who'd fail to earn Valorie's approval, which for some reason meant a lot to me.

But that night was different. As she predicted, I did meet someone. Andre had gone to elementary school with Valorie. Not only was he attractive but he seemed like a normal guy, nothing scary or threatening about him. When he asked me to dance, I agreed, although I kept hoping my hair wouldn't get messed up.

"Did you go to Crescent Heights too?" he asked.

"No, I met Valorie at JB." I explained.

"Can I get your number and call you later?"

I tried not to smile too much, but I was happy that Valorie had gone to all the fuss to make me look cute.

After we danced, Andre and I found a quiet corner and just talked. He was a really nice boy and told me again how pretty I was. We had fun! We danced and acted silly all night.

The party came to a close around one o'clock in the morning, *waaaay* past our curfew. Valorie and I were relieved that our lie had held up far better than my hair. My new party look was quickly fading . . . back to the real me.

"Everybody was lookin' at you, girl," said Valorie, as we walked back to my house in the dark. "Those girls I was talkin' to were so jealous."

"Really?" I asked.

"Yeah, girl. Didn't you know? Everybody wants to date Andre, and he danced with you all night!"

"He's super fine!"

As I put the key into the door of my apartment, we could already hear the phone ringing. By the time we got the door open, it was too late to answer it. As usual, no one was home at my house. We decided to change into our PJs, watch some TV, and get on the party line.

"Maybe Andre will call me tonight."

"You have a crush on Andre," she sang.

Though I didn't want to admit it, I was hoping that it was Andre who had called just a few minutes earlier.

The phone rang again.

"Oooo." I got so excited. "I hope it's Andre."

"Me, too!" Valorie said. "Answer it. Hurry up."

I picked up the phone and smiled. "Hello."

"Christa, this is Mama Shirley. I've been calling your house for hours to check on you."

I stood there with the phone in my hand, covering the receiver. I gulped and stammered, "It's . . . it's . . . your mom. Here, she wants to talk to you."

We'd been busted. Mama Shirley was extremely upset to find out that we had been left alone with no supervision. Even worse, that we'd been at Kelly's party—the very party Valorie had not been given permission to attend.

Valorie's mom made her pack her things immediately. "I'm on my way to get you right now."

Valorie wasn't allowed to spend the night at my house for many years after that.

Despite the consequences, Valorie and I still managed to bend the rules every now and then, even with supervision. Andre and I didn't become a thing—dating someone from a different school was the equivalent of being in a long-distance relationship, and that just didn't work for us. But I was okay with it because I soon met my first real boyfriend at JB.

Gordy was definitely from the wrong side of the tracks, and he didn't try to hide it. He was the coolest ninth grader at school. He was a bad boy from Compton, the area that would later be made famous by Ice Cube's movie *Straight Outta Compton*. He didn't try to hide the fact that he came from a family of street hustlers. It gave him a confidence that was different from the other guys at school. He was a man amongst boys.

I didn't know it at the time, but he had the gift of persuasion. He was notorious for smooth talking to all the girls at school. There were several of us that he whispered sweet nothings to in order to get our precious lunch money.

Like most other things in my life, I tried to keep my relationship with Gordy a secret. I fell for him, even though he was obviously too young and incapable of giving me the thing I was really looking for—the love of a father. How foolish of me . . . how naive.

Gordy's hustle was to sell ten-dollar bags of weed to the students at our junior high school. Somehow, he had managed to win the favor of campus security and they'd turn their heads while he'd make his money. I never asked how he had gotten a pass. I've always assumed freebies were part of the payoff.

Valorie hated Gordy. "He's a sneaky, low-life creep!" she'd say with disgust. "Why do you like him?"

I liked him because his attention was useful, almost vital, to me in those days. I was his girlfriend in his world of secrets, and I was best friends with Valorie in our normal teenage world. But when the two collided, well, it was awkward.

While I'd be hanging out in the quad with Valorie and other girls, Gordy would sometimes do things that embarrassed me.

"Uh, Christa?" asked Valorie one day in the middle of good gossip. "Why is Gordy always acting like he's Sherlock Holmes or something?" She thought he was spying on us or on me. "He looks like he's up to no good again."

Although it did bother me that she didn't like Gordy, in hindsight I realized that she was trying to look out for me—she knew he was trouble. She also knew that I could do better, but I had to discover that for myself. Despite her warnings, I went over to see what he wanted.

"Hey, Christa," said Gordy. "I need you to do me a favor and take this little package into the girls' bathroom. Give it to the girl with the red jacket on. She's going to give you ten dollars for me."

I wish I had told him to take his own "Mary Jane" into the bathroom and lose my number while he was at it! But that would come later. I'm not sure why I was so willing to put myself in jeopardy for him to make ten dollars, but at that age, I would have done anything to win his approval and attention.

Sadly, Gordy's criminal activities escalated. One day, he asked me to take a bus trip out to the Valley with him. And once again, I didn't hesitate or ask any questions.

It took us what seemed like two hours to arrive at our destination. We walked up to this really nice ranch-style home and rang the doorbell. I'd never actually been inside a house that nice before. It reminded me of the Brady Bunch; something you'd see on TV but not in real life.

A teenage Black guy answered the door and walked us back to his bedroom. "You got it?" he asked anxiously. "Let me see it."

Gordy pulled out a shiny black object and slapped it into his hand.

My eyes got big. *That's not weed*, I said to myself. *It's a gun.*

The exchange happened quickly. The boy got the gun, and Gordy got his money. I was quiet all the way back to the bus stop. It was one thing to sell weed, but guns were another story. Gordy, of course, acted like the gun exchange was no big deal.

It took us even longer to get back to LA because buses didn't run as frequently at night. I never asked Gordy about the switch from drugs to weapons. As a matter of fact, I never questioned him about anything he did. I admit, I was a little scared, but I felt secure because Gordy seemed to know how to handle himself. He was much more mature than the other boys at school, living as an adult despite his young age, and he filled the void where my father should have been.

When we got downtown, Gordy announced that he was getting off in a few stops. "I'll see you at school tomorrow."

"Wait," I said, looking out to the blackness of the night. "I don't think I know how to get home from here."

He stood up and pulled the cord. *Ding, Ding.* "This is my stop, man," he said to the driver and then turned to me. "Just stay on this bus then get off at the school. You'll know how to get home from there." And off into the dark he went.

I was scared. The people on the bus ride home were older. They weren't the students I was used to riding with in the mornings. In an area like Compton, darkness changed everything. The tired faces of the passengers seemed suspicious and sinister. I was desperately unprepared to navigate that journey solo.

10

THE PLAN

Over time, my circle of friends and surroundings shifted, yet the pain and despair that weighed on me never fully dissipated.

I had become an expert at hiding. No one, not even my best friend, knew how depressed I was. The relationship between Mama and me had grown even more dysfunctional and distant. I was constantly haunted by the absence of my father, and I grieved the loss of my siblings, a suffering that had yet to find voice. Even though I had my aunts, my cousins, Valorie, and her family, I often felt completely alone in the world.

I began to question everything, even asking, *Why was I born?* I wrestled with the burden of having ruined my mother's life. Because of me, she had been abandoned by the man she believed that she would spend the rest of her life with. Her own trauma consumed her—rendering her emotionally helpless. I could no longer depend on her for love or guidance. In essence, I had lost both of my parents. I began to feel overwhelmingly *hopeless*. If my future was going to look anything like the past, or even the present for that matter, then *what was the point in living?*

I began entertaining the idea of suicide. I'd seen a movie where someone tried to kill themselves by taking an overdose of aspirin only to wake up hours later in a Psych Ward. Clearly, if I was going to end it, I had to find a more effective option than Tylenol. So I began stealing my cousin's anti-seizure medicine. I made sure that I only swiped a few pills at a time so that no one would notice.

Forever etched in my memory is the night I made up my mind to carry out my plan. It was during Christmas break. The perfect storm included a big fight with Mama. That night, in the middle of the argument, she blurted out that she wished I had never been born. Her words broke me. I'd been angry with her for years, throwing all my pain toward her because it was the safest place it could land.

I resented her for being an absentee parent. I never understood why our relationship couldn't be normal. I hated her unpredictable behavior. I also hated the fact that she didn't fight fair. When she was angry, she was unpredictable. I never knew what might come out of her mouth. That night she had gone too far. No matter how remorseful she was, those were words that couldn't be taken back. And they echoed loud and clear the night I decided to put an end to it all.

I determined she'd be better off without me. I also thought my suicide might finally make her understand the level of pain she had inflicted on me. Selfishly, on some level, I may have even wanted to hurt her back. But ultimately, all I really wanted . . . all I had ever really wanted . . . was to be loved.

This is it, I said to myself. *No more; I'm gonna end me.*

Too numb to cry, I went into the bedroom and retrieved the stash of pills I'd been hiding in a drawer. Next, I went to the kitchen sink and got a big cup of water. Finally, I took a handful of the pills and started downing several at a time. I'd rehearsed this in my mind many times, but this night I followed through. I curled up on the living room sofa and waited for the welcomed moment of *"me no more."*

Anxious for death, I didn't even write a note, as I'd originally planned to do. *I'll just go to sleep and disappear. No one will care when I'm gone.*

The phone pierced the silence.

I lay there and let it ring. But the phone kept ringing. And ringing. I'm not sure why I decided to answer. Maybe just to stop it from annoying me. Whatever the reason, I picked up the receiver and quietly said, "Hello."

"Hey, what's up with you?" It was Gordy. "Were you sleeping?"

"No, I was just watching TV," I lied.

"I was calling to see what you've been up to." He explained that he'd been staying at his cousin's house over the break.

Then suddenly, I remembered. *Christa, you took those pills! What are you going to do?* In that moment, I knew I didn't want to die. I just didn't know how to live. I didn't feel like I'd ever really be able to have a happy, stable life. I was tired of all the drama. Tired of all the pain. Tired. I was tired.

Gordy kept talking.

So many thoughts floated around in my mind. Everything seemed to be happening in slow motion. Out of me came this desperate whisper, words that surprised me. "God, I don't want to die."

I told Gordy I'd call him back later. I raced to the bathroom, shoved my finger down my throat, and forced myself to throw up as much as I could. Feeling shaky, sad, and stupid, I lay back down on the couch. Only this time, my prayer became a tearful plea. "God, please don't let me die! If You get me out of this, I won't ever try to take my own life again."

I didn't know how I would find a way to make my life less painful. I just knew, in that moment, that I wanted to live. Self-preservation battled depression that night and won.

The next morning when I woke up, I knew that He had heard me. I'm not even sure why I cried out to Him that night. In that darkest moment, I believed that He could somehow rescue me.

I was sick for several weeks afterward, but I didn't dare tell a soul about my suicide attempt. It was a secret I would guard with my life. I didn't want anyone to think I was crazy.

During that time, I thought a lot about why I had decided to take my life in the first place. I also thought about Gordy's timely call.

11

I'M NOT CRAZY

For a short stint of time, I moved back in with my mama. One day, she barged into my room and very matter-of-factly announced, "Once a week, you'll be going to see my counselor."

With that, the door slammed behind her and my world changed yet again.

"Wait, what? I don't need to see a counselor," I said out loud to no one. *I'm fine.*

I hopped up from my bed and busied myself in my room. *I don't need to see no counselor. Counselors are for crazy people and I'm . . . well . . . I'm not crazy.*

Crazy carried a certain stigma with it. I had been through a lot in my life, but I was convinced that all the pain and trauma that had happened to me in my life, hadn't seriously impacted me. At least not enough to make me crazy. I was strong. A survivor. Even my dark thoughts of suicide seemed to be a thing of the past, since that fateful evening. Everything was fine . . .

I was upset at Mama for making me go to counseling without asking my opinion first. Counseling was her thing, not mine. I resolved within myself that she might be able to make me go, but I definitely wouldn't be opening up and telling a stranger my deepest and darkest secrets. I'd just sit there for my hour. I'd show her!

The long car ride to the San Fernando Valley to see Cathy the counselor was awkwardly silent. The years of neglect and abandonment had erected an impenetrable wall between Mama and me. I had vowed in my heart that I would never let her over that wall. I couldn't risk being hurt again.

True to my promise, I arrived at the first session with my cavalier attitude intact. I made sure to keep my I-don't-like-you-or-need-you face on for my mama *and* the counselor. No way were they going to break me.

Cathy, Mama's counselor, emerged from her office with a pleasant smile. The kind that made you instantly want to trust her. "Diane, come on back," She then turned to me and said, "Christa, I'm going to see your mother first, and then I'll come out and get you."

I sat in the lobby for what seemed liked hours, thumbing through stories in *Reader's Digest* and the tattered magazines from the waiting room table. This was a waste of my time. I could be hanging out with my friends and talking on the phone with Chuckie, the guy who'd replaced Gordy for a moment. We'd been in a *very serious* relationship for all of two weeks! Chuckie, I felt certain, was *the one*.

Running out of things to keep me busy, I played MASH, a fold-up paper fortune-telling game perfected by teens of the 1980s. MASH predicted if we were going to live in a mansion, apartment, shack, or house, along with how many children we would have. Although I don't recall the exact results, my future with Chuckie looked pretty bright according to the fates.

After about an hour, it was finally my turn to see Cathy without my mother. Surprisingly, I liked her, and my resolve quickly melted. I hated to admit it, but Cathy had a way of disarming me right from the start. There was something about her that felt calming and reassuring. She oozed love, acceptance, and compassion.

"What would you like to talk about, Christa?"

The question took me by surprise. "I-I don't know," I stammered. But eventually, I began to open up to Cathy. Looking back, Cathy afforded me the space to speak freely and to express my feelings. Something I hadn't been able to do with anyone. I wasn't aware just how much I needed a safe place to process my feelings. Or at least some of them, that is.

I still dreaded the long drive, but secretly, I had begun to look forward to talking with Cathy each week. Although, I still kept some of the deep dark stuff to myself. Like how I had become addicted to binging and purging my food. No matter how many times I promised myself that I wouldn't do it again, I was powerless to stop. I would continue to struggle with bulimia for years. I didn't have the courage to tell Cathy that I desperately wanted to fit in and to be accepted and that I'd do just about anything to do so. Those were just some of the things that I'd keep tucked tightly away.

I had been seeing Cathy for almost a year, when I finally built up the courage to talk to her about my father. I shared with her how I really missed not having a dad. His absence was a deep void that nothing seemed to fill. I felt worthless, like damaged goods. Why hadn't he stuck around to give me the things I needed most— his love and affirmation or his last name? I had so many unanswered questions about him. Did he ever think about me and wonder how I was doing? Did he have regrets about abandoning me and Mama? I didn't even know if he was still alive. Mama and I never spoke of him. It was as if there were a long-standing silent agreement between us. We never discussed my father or Norman, and never could we mention Hasan and Aisha.

I did know that I had red hair like my father, and that he was a priest. The rest I had to make up, which I often did. Sometimes, when I would pass an older White man, walking down the street, I would wonder to myself, *Is that what my father looks like?*

As with most counselors, I'm sure Cathy's intuition told her that I had to somehow be bearing the emotional consequences of my parents' relationship and of my father's decision to be absent from our lives. There was no way I could come out of this ordeal unscathed. She began asking me questions about my father in our sessions. Until one day she asked a question that caught me off guard.

"Christa, would you like to look for your father?"

I mean, was it really possible to find him?

"I may be able to help you locate your father's whereabouts. The counseling community is small, " she said. I didn't want to appear too eager, so I played it cool.

"I'll check into it," she promised, jotting a quick note on her writing pad.

I'm not sure why, but it hadn't ever dawned on me before that we could actually go looking for my father. I'd always imagined that he lived too far away. Perhaps, he even worked at the Vatican? There had to be a really important reason he'd never come back for me. Not a call, nor a letter, not so much as even a post card from him, in all these years.

I quickly forgot about our conversation that day. Perhaps it was my way of protecting myself from yet another disappointment. Our weekly visits continued but nothing more was mentioned about finding my father.

One afternoon, Cathy broke protocol and did something she had never done before. She asked for my permission to have Mama join our session. I did my best to hide the fact that I was not only taken off guard by the sudden change in our routine, but I was annoyed by it. It was one thing to spill my guts to Cathy, but being vulnerable with my mama . . . well, that was a whole different story.

What was Cathy thinking? Was she going to try to force us to talk? I hoped not, because I wasn't ready for all of that. She was a great therapist, but even Freud had his limitations.

I had made a lot of progress, but I didn't feel ready for a full-on confrontation with her. Mama fancied herself an amateur lawyer, and I was sure to lose any argument we might have.

Cathy began to explain. "Diane, I don't think Christa needs to come to see me anymore. She's been through a lot, but she's resilient. My professional opinion is, she's not crazy!"

At least, that was what I heard her say.

"I think she will be okay."

There it was. The confirmation that I was *not crazy*. Cathy confirmed what I had known all along.

It was a joyous moment—finally, I was free of the stigma.

12

IN PLAIN SIGHT

Several months had passed since I had my last counseling session with Cathy. Then, one afternoon, the phone rang. Being the typical fifteen-year-old that I was, I rushed to answer, hoping it would Valorie, calling to make plans.

"Hello?"

"Christa, I've got some news to share with you." I recognized the voice on the other end right away. After having spent time with Cathy in counseling, I'd come to trust her voice.

"Christa, with the help of a few friends in my network, I have located your father," she said. *And I waited.*

"He's been living in the LA area for a while."

I had forgotten all about Cathy's promise to look for my father. This call shook me. I wasn't sure how to respond. It was almost as if a bomb had exploded. *Living right here in LA this whole time?* This certainly was not the news I expected.

"Are you still there?" she asked.

"Yeah, I'm still here. I'm just a little . . . surprised is all."

"I reached out to some people who knew some people, to see if your father was interested in the two of you meeting. He's agreed, and so now it's up to you." After a long pause, she said, "Christa?"

I let the silence linger. I had so many mixed emotions about reuniting with my father. I'd rehearsed this scenario over and over in my mind, but I don't think I had ever really believed that this day would actually come.

"It's your decision, Christa." Cathy continued. "I'll let you think about it and call you back in a few days. I'll arrange the meeting if you decide you still want to go through with this. Of course, talk it over with your mom."

Cathy hung up. I sat there stunned. An avalanche of thoughts and emotions flooded my mind. I expected to feel excited, but instead I was feeling even more disappointed and angry. *Had I heard Cathy correctly? Had my father really been living right down the street from us? Well, of course I want to meet him,* I thought to myself. *I'm finally going to get the opportunity to confront him to his face and make him explain why he had abandoned us.*

That afternoon, I summoned the courage to share my news with Mama. I wasn't sure how she'd take it.

"Cathy called me today." I took a long intentional pause. She's located my father. He's been living right here in the LA area all these years." I never told her about my conversation with Cathy. She had no idea that I wanted to meet him.

It took Mama a few minutes to be able to respond. It was a blow we were both struggling to recover from. When she finally did speak, her voice trembled. "He abandoned us both—and you say he's been living right here this entire time?"

It shocked us to learn that my father had been so close, yet so far removed from our lives. Why hadn't he ever tried to contact us? I felt an anger rising inside of me again. I began to think about his absence all those years, and it hurt very deeply. *I'd like him to feel the pain that I've had to feel. And then double it. Give him back the hurt he caused us.*

That was at least what the less vulnerable version of me wanted, if only to protect myself from seeming weak and desperate. After all, I had convinced myself that I didn't need a father. I didn't want to need anyone. The truth of the matter was that, inwardly, I was a lost little girl who desperately wanted a father— her father. I ached for his love.

I had grown up my entire life believing that my birth was some sort of tragic accident. Wreaking havoc in the aftermath. Just maybe things were going to change now that I was going to meet my father.

My heart raced. *Could it really be true that my father was still alive? Maybe Cathy's friends had made a mistake?* The news was hard to digest. For years, I had created my own narrative for his absence, convincing myself that there was some important reason why he hadn't come looking for me.

This new development left me with more questions than answers. I had to agree to meet him, didn't I? What other choice did I have?

"Mama," I said, hoping she would take what I was about to say without losing her temper. "I've decided to go meet my father. Are you going to be okay with that?"

I'm sure she was torn, although she didn't protest. I think she knew that this was something I had to do. I had waited for this opportunity for many years. I had to go.

***

My father had been living in Hermosa Beach, a mere fifteen miles from us. Yet, he'd been lost to me for fifteen years! It had left me wondering if he'd ever tried to find us.

Even once?

He was no longer a priest, but he had continued to work with high school students, only in the public school system instead of a private Catholic school. The irony of it all, was *too much*. As we got closer to our meeting, I started having second thoughts. But I knew that we were at the point of no return. My father and I were meeting face to face after all these years. The last time he saw me, I was just a few months old. In a strange kind of way, I was afraid that my father might not approve of me. I'm not sure why that still mattered to me after all these years. I guess it was something my inner child still needed.

As I put on a little lip gloss and curled my hair. I stared at my reflection in the mirror. "Don't cry," I said aloud. "Whatever you do, be strong."

"Come on, Christa," said Mama with a knock on the bathroom door. "You don't wanna be late."

I checked the mirror one more time to make sure I looked okay. While Mama wasn't going with me, she did seem nervous as I left her to drive off to the meeting spot.

Cathy had arranged our meeting at another counselor's office—a neutral location. Ironically, the relationship between my parents had begun in counseling and here we were again.

My palms began to sweat, and my mouth felt dry, like the desert. Cathy led me into a small conference room, and for the first time in my life, I laid eyes on my father.

There he sat, in the flesh. *Yep, he's my father all right. We have the same dimple in our chins.* He was far older looking than my mother, certainly old enough to have known she was too young for him when she walked into his office at the age of fourteen. He'd been almost thirty when he met her. And well into his thirties when he drove to her apartment to satisfy his longings on her eighteenth birthday.

I studied him closely and realized that I had inherited my father's fair skin and his rather large ears, of all things. A beautiful woman, of Spanish or Mexican ancestry, sat next to him. I didn't have the courage to look him in the eyes, for fear that I'd lose it. Underneath the table my legs were shaking, and I could feel my lips quivering. I did everything within my power to hold back the tears that were already threatening to break wide open. It was all I could do not to run from the room.

"Hi," said the woman. "My name is Yolanda." She extended her hand to shake mine. "I'm John's wife. It's nice to meet you."

As if it were possible, my heart broke again. I can't recall what John, the man my mother had known as Father Chris, actually said in that moment. Although, I do remember that it wasn't the meeting I had secretly yearned for.

My father didn't jump up and grab me or hug me or tell me how he, too, had dreamed of this day. Instead, he sat at the opposite end of a long conference table and talked in sort of a matter-of-fact tone, as if he were giving a deposition.

The other counselor cleared his throat. "So, Christa, Cathy tells us you wanted to meet your father and that you may have some questions?"

Clearly, all eyes were on me, the broken-but-trying-to-be-strong teenager. I felt like I had been swept up by a strong current—the waves pulling me under and thrashing me around while I struggled to come up for air. It was difficult to take it all in.

My father finally spoke up and asked what grade I was in and how I liked school. I'd imagined that our reunion would have been more healing, more significant. Instead, it felt shallow to me—like asking *how's the weather been these past fifteen years?*

Yolanda was kind. I remember her saying something like, "Oh, Honey, it's okay. John makes me cry sometimes, too."

Oh my God! Am I crying? I took the tissue from her and quickly dabbed the tears from my face. She was trying really hard to make the awkwardness go away. She shared that she had two children prior to their marriage—two sons. And she told me their names and ages.

Wham! Her words fell on my heart like a hammer. It broke me to hear that John had been helping to raise someone else's children.

"We have one child together . . . another girl. Her name is Chrisna."

Chrisna?! Had he forgotten all about his firstborn daughter, named Christa? Had it been that easy to erase and replace me?

My mother had named me Christa because, back then, she really believed she and Father Chris had a future together. Of all the names my father could have chosen for her, why had it been so close to my name? Why had he loved his second daughter and not his first?

Something shifted inside my heart that day. A part of it turned cold, filling up with an intense feeling of resentment. I made a vow that day to never need or forgive my father. I could take no more rejection. I could carry no more pain. The hurt was now full-blown rage.

Almost as quickly as it had begun, our "session" was over. There would be no long goodbyes, no promises to meet again, no future for us as father and daughter. I left more broken that day than I had been when I came in. I was confused and hurt. And I was building a wall around my heart.

Before the meeting, I could at least pretend that he *wanted* to be a father to me. That he was out there somewhere loving me, missing me, planning for the day he'd find me.

But after meeting my father, the make-believe fantasy came to a crashing halt. I was left with the cold hard reality of the truth. *He doesn't want you, and he never has. You've been fooling yourself all these years, Christa.*

Later, when I described the meeting to Mama, her expression shifted from concern for me to anger, saying all the words I couldn't.

"How dare he love and support some other woman's kids, after abandoning us and leaving us to fend for ourselves in the Jungle!"

Without any need for explanation, my mother gave her head one quick nod and said, "He can't get away with this. I won't let him!"

By that time, she'd already taken a few law classes at a community college in Los Angeles. With a passion for social justice, she was on a new mission. Someone had to right all the wrongs being done to people. Why not her?

What Father Chris did not know was that my mother had become more courageous since he'd taken advantage of his vulnerable student. Having endured so many injustices in her life—financially, emotionally, physically, spiritually, and educationally—she was now outspoken!

She'd become an activist, a crusader who would focus the microscope and teach the world to recognize the wrongdoings going on right under their noses. But now her passion had been directed to a new cause—holding men like my father . . . and her father . . . responsible for the damage they'd done.

She began to write letters to politicians in Sacramento, and I accompanied her to a hearing on absentee fathers. She lobbied to see changes take place with child support laws. She even had the courage to confront the Catholic Church with her truth. She wrote a letter to the diocese, explaining our plight.

*We've been living in abject poverty all these years. My daughter
and I had no one to turn to for help . . .*

But despite her pleas to the leaders in the Church, the DA, and
powerful law makers, everyone brushed her away, not wanting to get
involved in such a controversial matter involving a priest.

It was clear to my mother what we needed to do to rectify the
wrongs. She took my hand and said, simply, "We'll find someone to
help us sue him for back child support. He owes us."

The adage is true: "Hurt people, hurt people." I made the
decision that if I ever had the chance to help Mama seek revenge
against my father, I would.

And it would be purely out of spite.

13

SIXTEEN CANDLES

Moving around was our norm. My mother and I moved countless times for various reasons. Sometimes the reasons were financial, and at other times our moves were because she needed fresh emotional space.

The constants in my life had always been my mother's sisters, Vicky and Fern. While my mother's place was my foundation, it wasn't always a steady one, so I bounced around a lot and never complained when I landed back with my aunts. Fern and Vicky were funny and nurturing, and they offered me a stable, safe place in the midst of many uncertainties.

Even with all of the surrogate mothering, gifts, meals, and day trips, deep down I resented not having my own parents as consistent sources of love in my life. I would always feel sad during the holidays and other major life events. I'd mourn my birthdays because I'd be reminded of the havoc my birth had wreaked on my mother's life; an event that had brought her far too much loss and hardship. I grew to hate the day I was born. September 1, 1967, had not been a day of celebrating, and September 1, 1983—my sixteenth birthday—was sure to be no different.

A few months before I would turn sixteen, I ended up moving back in with my Aunt Vicky—she still lived in her small two-bedroom, one-bath apartment in the Jungle. Although she was barely getting by, she was willing to make room for me once again.

"Christa," said Aunt Vicky, with a welcoming arm around my shoulders to cheer me up. "We'll fix up the dining room and make it your spot."

My cousins didn't seem to mind that I was back. Over the years, we had all grown accustomed to living in cozy, tight quarters. My aunt knew how to make the best out of even the most difficult situations. We were family, and they stuck by me when I needed them most.

There is a saying that "Some folks know how to make a dollar out of fifteen cents." Well, one of my ancestors must have written that proverb, because we learned to stretch money a lot in our family.

My Aunt Vicky was a curvy, sassy spitfire who "didn't take *no mess* from anybody." She was a few years older and had way more street smarts than my Aunt Fern—who was the baby in their family.

Although living with Aunt Vicky was sorta like an extra-long sleepover, I'd have to get a job in order to help carry my load. I was very aware that I was another mouth to feed, although I never heard her complain about my having to live with her.

Things were tight financially, so my cousins and I always looked forward to payday. It meant that the refrigerator would be full for at least a week or two. It also meant that my aunt would cook some of her favorite meals.

"I'm in the mood for some enchiladas," she'd say.

She made the best enchiladas! Her enchiladas had a soul food twist and tasted far better than any we could find at the local Mexican food spot, not that we could have afforded to dine at a restaurant anyway. She taught me her secret recipe, and I still enjoy cooking them today.

Aunt Vicky shared her home, love, recipes, and life experiences with an open heart. She also tried to teach me to be street smart.

"When I was in my younger years, they called me Annie Oakley," Aunt Vicky boasted, explaining that Annie Oakley was a folk hero, a tough woman of the Wild West who was best known for her sharp shooting skills. My aunt began to tell me the story of a time when her ex-husband made the mistake of trying to push her around.

"There's a thin line between love and hate," she said, chuckling.

They had met and married young and while they'd loved each other, their relationship seemed to be plagued by many issues.

"One time, while we were separated, he came over to my place and threatened to put his hands on me. I had something for him that day."

Her story reminded me of Sofia, a character in Alice Walker's book, *The Color Purple*. Sofia, later played by Oprah Winfrey in the movie, was not the type of woman who was going to take a beatin' lyin' down, and neither was Aunt Vicky.

"He got a surprise when he came to my house that day," she continued. "I was ready for him. I had gotten a shotgun." She smiled and squinted, as though she were a villain on TV. "Mr. C, if you come one step closer, I'll shoot your black—!"

My mouth fell open at the expletive that followed. Was my sweet, sassy, cooler-than-cool aunt really capable of shooting somebody?

"Christa, you have to stand up for yourself. Otherwise, people will think that you are weak and they will try to take advantage of you."

I'm not sure if her story had been embellished, but it didn't matter. I respected her, and I admired her strength. I wanted to be strong and fearless, like she was.

That summer was spent working. A friend told me that a theater in Hollywood was hiring and encouraged me to apply. Only this wasn't a theater that showed the latest summer blockbuster movies. The Pantages Theater featured Broadway plays and hosted music concerts. I interviewed and got the job, which meant that I'd be able to save up some money.

Being an usher turned out to be a great job. I got to see Phil Collins perform some of his greatest songs live: "In the Air Tonight," "Against All Odds (Take a Look at Me Now)," "One More Night," and "Sussudio."

Working at the Pantages gave me opportunities that would not have otherwise been afforded to me. I had the opportunity to see Yul Brynner perform to sold-out audiences in Rodgers and Hammerstein's *The King and I*, for which he'd won two Tony Awards. Over the course of his career, he played the role 4,625 times onstage, and supposedly never gave a bad performance. I knew all the songs from the play by heart.

On one of my shifts, I received word from my manager that a very special guest would be sneaking in to watch Brynner perform. The house lights went down and one of my friends ushered Michael Jackson to his seat. Wow! Michael Jackson was an icon, and I had gotten almost close enough to touch him. This was the same year he released his infamous music video "Thriller." A group of friends and I didn't mind paying the full three-dollar ticket price to see it even though it was only fourteen minutes long.

Before I knew it, I was beginning my senior year of high school. The job had been so fun, I couldn't believe how quickly the summer had ended. The theater had given me a peek at an outside world, something far bigger and more glamorous than anything I'd seen in my world. If I didn't know anything else about my life, I knew I wanted more than a life in the Jungle. But in order to get there, I'd need to go to college.

In spite of the gaps in our living arrangements, my mother's words about the importance of getting an education always seem to reverberate in the back of my mind. She continued dabbling in a college class here and there, but her real dream had still eluded her. I know she wanted to wear the title of "college graduate." Instead, she was still trapped in low-paying secretarial jobs that had never allowed her to reach her fullest potential. I was always reminded that her dreams had been put on hold for so long by so many, and I was determined not to let her sacrifices go to waste.

"You're smart, Christa. Just like me," she'd say. "A good degree will open up doors for you."

Her advice stuck with me.

Jobs for a sixteen-year-old were scarce, so I kept working at the Pantages Theater throughout my senior year in high school. I still didn't own a car, so I relied on public transportation, as I'd done since I was young. The time changed and bright summer nights dulled into winter darkness, with the sun sinking low each night around five thirty. Sometimes it would be close to midnight before I'd make it back to The Jungle after my shift.

"Christa," said Aunt Vicky, concerned. "You've been getting home really late."

"I know. I hate it, but I haven't been able to get a job closer to home." I explained.

"Well, you need to carry some protection," she said handing me a little pocket knife. "Just in case someone tries to mess with you on the bus," she warned.

I wasn't sure how a small pocket knife could protect me. Nonetheless, I took her advice, tucking the little blade into my purse in case I ever needed it.

One late night after work, a man struck up a conversation with me at the bus stop.

"Hey, hey! How you doin'?" His breath reeked of liquor, so I stepped aside.

"Fine, thanks." I quickly retorted. I didn't make eye contact with him, hoping he'd get the hint. *It's too late to be talkin' to anybody. Leave me alone,* I thought to myself.

He didn't seem to read the vibe. "Where you headed this late?"

"Home," I said, tersely.

"Me, too. I live over by Dorsey. How about you?"

Dorsey High School was several stops past my street. By no means was I going to say where I lived. I knew better.

The bus pulled up and I got on. The annoying stranger left me alone and went to the back of the bus. I sat up front so I could be next to the driver and could get off quickly.

"Hillcrest Drive, young lady," the driver said. "Good night! I'll see you tomorrow."

"Good night."

As the door closed, and the bus drove away. I suddenly sensed someone behind me.

"Hey sweetness," he called out. "Wait up. We can walk together to our cribs."

It was the man who'd been trying to talk to me earlier. He'd said he lived a mile or so past me. *Why did he get off at my stop?*

I slid my hand into my purse and gripped the handle of the knife just like I had been instructed to. It frightened me to think that I might actually have to use it. I didn't know if I had the courage to harm another human being.

I could hear my aunt's voice say, "You have to protect yourself, Christa."

I argued back with the voice in my head. *Please don't make me do it.* In that moment, it seemed to me as if something or someone was now with me, protecting me. The man suddenly stopped following me and walked on across the street. I was safe. Thank goodness I didn't have to use that knife.

***

I'd live with Aunt Vicky through my entire senior year of high school. My plan was to get accepted to college and move into the dorms in the fall, but for now I still lived in The Jungle. I was one of the lucky ones though; at least I had options—in just a few short months, I'd be leaving my life in the Jungle behind.

One of the perks of being a senior was that we would have a lighter school schedule. It also felt good to be a part of the popular group. By default, we had earned the respect of the underclassmen by paying our dues when we were young, naive freshman.

As soon as the semester began, we all came down with a bad case of *senior-itis*. My friends and I were already beginning to reminisce about the events that the year held. A few of us sat around discussing what we were going to wear to the senior ball, and plotting the excuses we were going to give school administrators when we skipped school for the highly anticipated Senior Ditch Day. On Senior Ditch Day, most of our classmates planned to play hooky and head to the Santa Monica Boardwalk. It was supposed to be one of the highlights of that year; something we'd waited four years to experience.

That semester, I planned to take my first music class. As much as I'd grown up loving to sing, I had never taken a music class or a voice lesson. Now I'd be participating in our school choir. I assumed we wouldn't be performing any of the R&B songs I was used to, but I was ecstatic just to be singing with a real group. Until then, I'd sung solo in the bathroom mirror (or with Valorie in impromptu living room performances). This was definitely going to be different.

In choir, I met an interesting guy named Antoine. He had a deep, smooth voice like Barry White, only he was tall, skinny, and not at all sexy. He fit better in the Steve Urkel category, but he was a kind soul. We also had history class together that year, which meant we'd spend a lot of time hanging out. We made a connection almost instantly, but it wasn't romantic. Instead, our connection was purely musical. Antoine introduced me to a few girls who sang—they shared the same passion that I had, only they were way more experienced.

When Antoine sat down at the piano and played, he ignited the room with his soulful sound. I was taken aback by his talent. I'd never met anyone who could play the piano like him, especially at our age.

"Where'd you learn to play and sing?" I asked.

"Oh, I've been doing this my whole life," he said, as if his talent was insignificant. "I've grown up singing in the choir and playing the piano at my church. Nothing special." He showed a great deal of humility. "If you want to hear some real singing, you should come with me to Cornerstone Institutional Baptist Church. Reverend Cleveland and his choir are amazing!"

Uh . . . Who? What? I thought to myself. *Institution?* That was a mouthful. Funny. Antoine seemed to think that I knew who James Cleveland was. I didn't want him to know that I had no clue what he was talking about, so I nodded politely.

"Oh, yeah, sure, maybe I'll do that."

Our relationship was unique. I'd never had a guy friend before. Prior to meeting Antoine, I was completely unaware that there was church music that sounded like the R&B stuff I loved listening to and performing. He opened a new avenue for me to explore and to appreciate.

Antoine and I spent just about every day together that semester. We'd catch up on the weekend's events as we walked from history to choir, and sometimes we'd even ride the bus home together.

Mostly, we talked about school and how we were looking forward to graduation. As we became closer friends, we'd share more personal things about our lives outside of class. I knew he spent a lot of time at church, but I didn't really know what that entailed. I also knew he had a girlfriend. One day he showed me a picture of her. She was pretty. The two of them had met in church and she also sang at the Institution. They'd been together for several years.

Antoine and I were as opposite as two people could be, yet we were friends. I'm not sure why, but one day while we were having one of our usual discussions about life and plans after high school, I suddenly blurted out, "I think I might become a minister when I grow up."

It shocked Antoine almost as much as it shocked me. But who better to have let something like this slip out to? He was the only real religious person I knew.

Where had that come from? I wondered. I don't think I even really knew what a minister did. I certainly didn't know any ministers, since we weren't the church-going type at all.

"Uh, women aren't ministers," Antoine replied. "But they can become deaconesses."

"What's that?" I asked.

"It's what the women who serve in the church are called," he answered.

"Okay, then I'm going to be a deaconess, or whatever you call it."

Antoine didn't argue, but I'm sure he must have said to himself, *Ha! That ain't gon' happen.*

"You should know," he said, "They don't let folks who cuss, drink, and smoke serve in church."

We walked to class with the church rules weighing in my head.

Later that week, Antoine introduced me to a friend of his named Bridgette. She was an old soul who seemed to have long outgrown high school.

"I'm just biding my time," Bridgette told me. "As soon as I graduate, I'm outta here. I'll be traveling and singing."

I had no reason to doubt her. Bridgette had one of the most amazing voices I'd ever heard. She had a mellow jazz sound that made you wanna listen. When Antoine and Bridgette sang together, they were like Lionel Richie and Diana Ross. Pure magic!

Antoine played piano, Bridgette sang, and I listened. The two were preparing to audition for the graduation performance.

On a whim, I decided to secretly sign up for the tryouts as well.

I'd only get two minutes to make an impression on the panel of judges. I chose to sing Barbra Streisand's "The Way We Were." I loved that movie starring her and Robert Redford.

He was F-I-N-E fine!

They made auditions look so easy on the TV show *Fame*—where all the students went to New York City's School of Performing Arts. But singing in front of people, especially ones who were critiquing you, rattled my confidence. I calmed my nerves by pretending I was singing to Robert Redford instead of the judges. Unleashing my fears for a moment, I let out a soulful cry, my voice echoing through the empty auditorium, as I poured my soul into the music.

As the last note faded away, one of the judges turned to me with a smile. "Thank you," she said warmly.

"What's your name again? You're an amazing talent. Why haven't you auditioned for any of our plays before?"

I struggled to frame a response. The truth was that I hadn't known the drama department even existed. What's more, I didn't have time to get involved in extracurricular activities. While other kids danced and sang, I worked to help to pay for the things I needed, like bus fare and money to wash my clothes.

My mom had concocted a plan for me to work long before I was of the legal age to do so. She was always looking for ways to beat the system and for us to survive. All it took was a typewriter and a little Wite-Out to forge my birth certificate and *voila!* I was now old enough to get a workers permit. The forgery landed me my first job, working at McDonald's. I worked most days after school, which prevented me pursuing anything fun, like being in an actual play.

"I would have loved to have a voice like yours in our musical *Little Shop of Horrors*," said the judge. "Check back in a few days. We'll post our selection on the auditorium door."

A few days later, as we were heading to choir class, several students were standing by the choir room door, checking to see if they'd been selected to sing for graduation. One by one, they were turning away with expressions of disappointment. I was nervous. I didn't want to check the list in front of Antoine, so I excused myself to the restroom. I was pretty sure that he and Bridgette had been selected. After all, they really were amazing.

I returned from the restroom, to find Antione and Bridgette jumping up and down, chanting.

"We did it!" said Bridgette. "Can you believe it? They selected us! Maybe we'll get to sing our arrangement."

She crooned, "*Lord, lift us up where we belong.*"

"You mean *love* lift us up where we belong?" I asked.

"Well, Antoine and I learned the gospel version in church, the one by BeBe and CeCe Winans," Bridgette explained. I had only heard the version from the movie, *An Officer and a Gentlemen.*

Little had I known, the two best singers in our school had *both* been trained in their church choirs!

I congratulated them and truly felt happy for the chance they'd have to spotlight their talents.

But then something unexpected happened. Bridgette had a mishap in one of her classes, which made her ineligible to sing at the graduation. Somehow the honor fell to me. In a few short months, Antoine and I would be singing, *"Love, lift us up where we belong"* at UCLA's Pauley Pavilion, in front of a few thousand people. School administrators were disapproving of the religious lyrics, so he and I sang the movie version instead.

14

WAR ZONE

It was a typical Wednesday evening, only I had the night off from work. It was rare for me to be home watching TV while my Aunt Vicky made dinner.

The phone blared out, as if to signify that there was an emergency.

"What?" The shrillness in her voice rendered me silent. "I don't understand. Who is this? Where are you?" She hung up the phone and scribbled a note on the back of a bill.

I rarely saw Aunt Vicky afraid, but this time I could smell fear in the air.

"Who was that?" I asked.

"Some woman," she said, methodically turning off the stove, then grabbing her purse and keys as she rushed toward the front door. "She said your cousin Gary is at her house and we need to get over there right away."

We hopped in her little red Mazda and headed over to this stranger's address.

Gary—just a year younger than me—had been forced to make a decision most young Black men from my 'hood had to make:

choose to become a hermit in the apartment, dare to go outside to get beaten up, or declare at least an affiliation to the very gang that would terrorize him if he didn't join them.

With dismal options, he did as many others had done. He chose to affiliate.

The ride across town felt like forever. The woman on the phone was in a panic and had only given my aunt sketchy details of that evening's events. All we knew was that there had been trouble. We still didn't know exactly what had happened to my cousin but, from the sound of her voice, we knew it wasn't good. There exists this code of ethics in the 'hood that everyone is forced to follow. *You gotta be aware of your surroundings at all times.* In our neighborhood, ignorance is not bliss. It could get you killed.

I reflected on my cousin's transformation. He had to at least play the game in order to survive.

Your clothing had to change and sometimes your language had to change too.

We lived in Blood territory. Bloods wore red. The color of their rival gang, the Crips, was blue. Bloods *never* wore *blue*.

I know it's hard for people who haven't lived this to understand. Why would anyone choose to become a part of something that is destined to cut your life short? All too often, we would hear about young men who had lost their lives because they were in the wrong place at the wrong time. But gang life is an enigma. It becomes the violent surrogate family that boasts belonging, offering a brotherhood and a sense of protection in a very volatile and dangerous world.

Aunt Vicky jerked the car to a stop. Although we didn't realize it at the time, we were smack dab in the middle of a Crip neighborhood. Unknowingly, we were thrust into a battle we were ill-equipped to fight—lambs for the slaughter.

After parking up the street, we exited the car and ran up to the vulnerable-looking house.

A frail Black woman scanned the street with eyes of fear before letting us in. We were horrified. My cousin Gary lay on her front room floor, bloody, pantless, and moaning from a face so badly beaten that he was unrecognizable.

Immediately, I knew what Gary's mistake had been. He had stepped into a war zone wearing the wrong color.

Aunt Vicky lost it. "We've got to get him to a hospital! Get the car!"

On her command, I rushed out to get the car without any real plan—all but oblivious to a car full of shadowy figures, slowly driving down the street, with their headlights turned off.

I jumped into the Mazda and pulled as close to the house as I could. We needed to get Gary to the hospital fast.

The woman kept repeating the same thing over and over. "He just crawled up to the door and cried, 'Help me.'" She was in shock.

Gary, now in my aunt's arms on the floor, was mumbling, but we couldn't make out what he was saying.

"Okay, I helped you guys," said the woman, anxiously. "You better go now."

Out of the corner of my eye, I saw two small children peek out from the small opening of a bedroom door.

"I-I don't want to be involved," she said. "Please, just go!"

"Involved in what?" I asked.

She never answered.

She kept going over to the big picture window in her living room and looking out, while motioning us to go. It struck me that she wasn't standing directly in front of the window, but instead was peering out from the side.

I went over to see what she was looking at. I walked right up to the window to get a plain view.

"Christa, get away from the win—" My aunt Vicky hadn't even finished getting the word out of her mouth when all of a sudden, *Pop! Pop! Pop!*

It sounded like the Fourth of July. Shards of glass littered the carpet as the house was sprayed with bullets.

We all hit the floor and scrambled toward the back of the house. We sat in a huddled mass; sharp fragments of glass had shot in every direction. Each of us was frantically breathing hard and trying not to cry out loud. The children were whimpering and clinging to the woman who had let us into her home. Somehow, we had managed to drag Gary into the room with us.

"Shut the lights off," someone whispered in all the commotion.

Silence filled the room as we waited. I feared that the shooters were going to kick the door in and finish the job. They seemed determined to kill my cousin, and maybe even us in the process.

I threw up a foxhole prayer. "Please don't let us die," I cried. "Please, God, don't let them kill us."

It was then that I felt a warm sensation on my back. I reached back and felt something wet and warm oozing from beneath my jumpsuit. "I've been shot."

"You haven't been shot," someone said. "Be quiet. They might hear us."

Just then, we heard a loud noise coming from the living room. I shook in fear as the men's voices moved through the small house.

Oh, no. *This is it!* I thought. Flashlight beams raced across the floor and up the walls.

No one dared make a sound.

Then, an answered prayer.

"LAPD! Anybody back here?"

We breathed a collective sigh of relief as an officer came to the back bedroom where we were hiding.

"Anyone hurt?" The officer's eyes fell on Gary.

"Help him," pleaded Aunt Vicky. "Please, help my son."

"I think I've been sh-shot." I stammered.

He blew me off. "You're just shaken, but you're okay now," he told me. "You're all safe.

We're here."

"It's burning," I said. "Can you just check?"

He shone his flashlight at my back and noticed what I later discovered was a small hole in my jumpsuit.

"You *have* been shot."

Why did he sound so surprised?

Although I wasn't in much pain, I started to cry. "I've really been shot?" The truth sank in. "Am I going to die?"

"You're going to be okay," he assured me, turning his attention back to Gary. "Medics, back here! We've got two victims."

The emergency responders came in the back room and put my cousin on a stretcher. Then they carried me out behind him. By that time, several cop cars had pulled up to the woman's house. Red lights flashed everywhere. Neighbors stood in their front yards trying to see the cause of all the gunfire. Like a scene out of a movie, shell casings had been strewn all over the lawn.

The ambulance ride was just as technical, sterile, and rushed as it was scary. *We'd been involved in a shooting. I couldn't believe this was really happening to us.* It was hard to process everything that had taken place. But we were all *alive*!

At the hospital, one of the paramedics gave a nurse a brief report of the events that had changed my life, and then he disappeared. Just like that, they were on their way to the next victim, most likely from another gunshot.

I was wheeled down the hall for an X-ray. Gary was taken to another wing of the emergency department.

Thirty minutes or so passed, while I waited to learn what sort of damage the bullet had done. A young ER doctor pulled back the thin hospital curtain . . . the only thing that separated me from the person in the bed to my left. "Hello, I'm Doctor London," he said pinning up the X-ray film on the screen in front of him. He stared at it for few moments with a very puzzled look on his face, until finally he delivered the news. "Today must be your lucky day," he said, pointing to the area on the the X-ray where the bullet had entered my back.

"I couldn't determine where the bullet exited, but there's no internal bleeding or damage. We won't have to do any surgery. Going in to try to find the bullet," he concluded, "could only make matters worse."

Whew! I breathed a sigh of relief and thought, *I'm going to live.*

Somehow the bullet has missed all of my vital organs. If a bullet remained inside me, I'd just have to live with it.

I was released a few hours later. To this day, I still wear a small scar resembling a cigarette burn on my back, a reminder that I had somehow cheated death.

My cousin Gary had to spend several painful days in the hospital due to the severe injuries he'd sustained to his face and jaw. His jaw had to be wired shut for several weeks which meant he couldn't really talk or eat. While his physical scars would eventually heal, the emotional ones would stick with him for years to come.

We had grown up hearing plenty of stories about kids dying early—but I don't think either of us had ever imagined we could become one of those statistics. As the doctor said, we were fortunate. Gary had almost been beaten to death and was left for dead. Thanks to the Good Samaritan who bravely opened her door and helped him, my young cousin survived.

The same evening, the police questioned a group of men they suspected had been involved in the shooting. They discovered evidence to connect them to the crimes that had been committed against us that night.

A year or so later, Gary and I were called to testify. However, neither of us were able to identify any of the suspects because we hadn't seen their faces. The DA's case was mostly circumstantial, and without a positive identification, they couldn't really hold anyone accountable. The suspects all got off with a slap on the wrist.

As much as we would have liked to have seen justice, Gary and I were both thankful we never actually had to testify against them in court. In our culture, *snitches get stitches and wind up in ditches,* which would mean putting ourselves in serious danger—again!

15

ROOMIES

My mere existence presented a peculiar contradiction. While my birth had completely turned my mother's world upside down, it also gave her something to be proud of. By choosing to give me life, instead of aborting me, she had done something good, something right. It took a lot of courage to be a single mom at a time when to do so meant being shunned by your community, your family, and even the church. It was even more audacious for her to raise me on her own without any emotional or financial support from my father, or anyone else, for that matter.

My mother took advantage of every opportunity to brag about me to her friends at work or to anyone who would listen.

She was especially proud of the fact that I would be graduating from high school and entering college at seventeen. Her ambition, as of late, was to graduate from UCLA. It didn't matter to her if she had to take one class at a time. She was willing to do whatever it took, so long as she could cross that finish line and graduate...a goal she had set for herself way back in high school, before she lost her innocence.

I wouldn't admit it, but hearing my mother brag about me to her friends bolstered my self-confidence. It felt like someone was pouring honey on my insides. It went down smooth and sweet!

Affirmation was on a slow drip in my life. I didn't even let it bother me that her compliments were sometimes laden with comparisons and personal accolades for herself. My mother needed a little honey in her life too. We both welcomed an extra boost of self-esteem, no matter the source.

After graduating from high school, I thought I'd give our relationship another try, so I decided to move back in with Mama. Aunt Vicky's place had been a refuge, but I felt it was time to give her and my cousins their space. I was optimistic that things could be different this time.

Every now and again, when things felt overwhelmingly hard between us, I would go and cry on Aunt Fern's shoulder. However, I made sure that those occasions were few and far between. Admitting that I needed people to help me was the same as declaring weakness in my mind. I couldn't afford to reside in that place too long.

That year or so I had spent in counseling with Cathy had helped me, but it had done very little to bring healing to Mama's and my relationship—a chasm of hurt still lay between us. It had long kept us from being close, so we settled on coexistence.

"Christa, now that you've graduated from high school, we can be more like roomies," she said. "Won't that be great? Don't worry, since you and I will be sharing the living expenses, I'm gonna treat you like I would a real roommate."

Nothing felt right about that to me. I didn't want to be roommates. I didn't want my privacy. I wanted a mother who would ask the nosy, invasive questions: *Where are you going? Who are you going with?* I envied the mother-daughter relationships my friends had. No matter their differences, they could still turn to their moms for advice and support. I wanted her to teach me how to navigate life, to handle relationships, to process my pain . . . but I would have settled for crumbs.

An occasional mother-daughter shopping trip or movie night . . . anything would have meant the world to me. But that type of relationship wasn't to be. It wasn't her fault. She couldn't really give me what she had never received herself.

So, I had no other choice—I was forced to adjust my expectations and accept our new relationship as *roomies*. As roommates do, we divided up the apartment. My mother lived her life, and I lived mine.

Sometimes our worlds collided. When they did, it would either be volatile or comical. There wasn't much of an in-between for us. I still hadn't gotten over the fact that she'd asked me to start paying rent in the first place. I had hoped that this time we would finally have a mother-daughter relationship. I was not interested in autonomy, but she was resolved that we would be *roomies* in every sense of the word.

She pushed my buttons when she would talk about my independence as her parental badge of honor. In her mind, she had been teaching me how to be a survivor. In my mind, she had been abdicating her parental responsibilities since I was a little girl. It's one thing to teach your child how to tie their shoes or cross the street without help, but it's another thing altogether to allow them to raise themselves. We were never going to see eye to eye on this subject. And no matter how hard I tried to fight it, I resented her.

One Saturday morning, Mama announced that she had special plans. "Are you going to work anytime soon?"

I thought it was an odd question to be asking so early in the morning. "No, I'm off today," I said, rubbing my eyes. I had barely managed to brush my teeth and tame my lion's mane of hair. "Why?"

"I'm having company over, and I need you to either stay in your room or be gone from the apartment for an hour."

So much for being respectful roommates. It was times like this that made me wonder if living with Mama was such a good idea after all. Her unpredictability was always hard for me growing up, and it was becoming obvious to me that I was not healed from the past. Though I really wanted things to work out between us this time, I couldn't shake the feeling that we were better off living apart.

Since I wasn't prepared to leave on such short notice, I opted to stay in my room instead.

Thirty minutes or so later, I heard an unusual sound coming from the living room. Although I'd agreed to give her privacy, curiosity got the best of me. I pressed my ear to my bedroom door as tightly as I could, trying to figure out what my mother was up to. I carefully cracked open the door, but I still couldn't figure out what was going on. *Are they speaking a foreign language?*

The volume of the voices went up and the tempo got stronger. "Hare Rama! Hare Rama! Rama, Rama, Hare, Hare!"

I peered through the small opening to witness the sight of my mother repeating the Maha Mantra, a common practice for the devotees of the Hare Krishna religious sect. I couldn't believe my eyes. I had seen them at the mall before, but I'd certainly never expected to find them standing right in our living room! But there they were, alongside my mother, in their bright orange garb and honoring Rama.

I didn't know much about religious rules of etiquette or best spiritual practices, but I was convinced that they must be breaking some sort of rules. I had encountered this group on the streets, and they'd always seemed harmless enough. I didn't feel any need to "rescue" my mother, so I left her to the chanting, and I closed my door, understanding that Mama was still searching for something bigger in her life, as most of us are.

By that afternoon, a large rectangular paper box had been erected on the wall of our living room. The shrine to Rama would remain there for many years. I was just glad Mama hadn't shaved her head!

16

THE CITY OF
TREES

September of 1984, Cindy Lauper's "Time after Time" blared on the radio as I drove an hour and a half in bumper-to-bumper traffic. Destination: California State University, Dominguez Hills.

Almost immediately, I began to regret my decision to stay in LA.

Dominguez was a commuter school. There were no bustling crowds of students rushing to class, no groups chatting or laughing in the quad— my social life looked pretty dismal. It didn't have the lively, college campus feel I'd hoped for. I had always imagined myself living in the freshmen dorms, but my student aid check dictated otherwise. The harsh reality was that I couldn't afford it. Instead, I'd have to face the disappointment of living at home with Mama, at least for awhile.

Dominguez was the college experience my grades afforded me. All the moving around, and the trauma I experienced during my high school years, made life complicated. Some days I was just too exhausted both emotionally and physically to engage. Although I'd been more than capable of achieving a 4.0 GPA, I was narrowly accepted into college with a 2.0.

And yet . . . I was still one of the fortunate ones! Most of the teens from my neighborhood wouldn't be able to go to college at all. A large percentage of them would never even graduate from high school, and far too many would have their lives cut short due to gang violence.

Midway through my freshman year, I decided I would definitely be transferring to a different college in the fall. I didn't know where I'd be going, but I knew I wasn't staying put at Dominguez for four years.

Since Mama and I were roommates, it only seemed right to give her notice that our living situation would soon be coming to an end. She didn't seem to mind my moving out at all; she had a potential roommate lined up to take my place.

A few months later, I received notice that Sacramento State University had accepted my transfer. It seemed as good a place as any for someone trying to escape a former life. I didn't know anyone who lived in Sacramento, but I didn't let that stop me. Being raised independently did have its benefits. It gave me the sense of confidence that I could survive *anywhere*. I had survived growing up in LA, but I was tired of living in a city where I constantly had to look over my shoulder. Sacramento was my way out. My way to a better life.

That summer, I loaded up my Ford Fiesta with the few possessions I owned. I shared goodbyes with all my family and Valorie, who had remained my best friend since our middle school days. I promised to call when I got settled in Sacramento and assured everyone I'd be back for Christmas break. I drove away, heading north.

I hadn't expected Sacramento to be so different from LA. Life in So Cal was edgy and fast paced. Sacramento was laid back and slow. Parts of Sacramento still had farms and cow pastures, reminding me of the summer trip I had taken to Alabama as a kid. Sacramento was nicknamed "The City of Trees." Trees grew in abundance in all directions. The air was fresh, and the skies were blue, unlike LA, where a constant gray haze of smog hung over the city.

I quickly adapted and settled in at Sac State. Calls home to Mama were infrequent. I tried to stay connected as I had promised, but our phone conversations felt even more clumsy and uncomfortable since the move. We still hadn't learned how to communicate with one another well.

I missed my aunts and cousins and hanging out at Venice Beach with Valorie. I also missed Sunday morning brunch with her family. The distance made it hard to keep up with one another, but when we did talk, we'd stay on the phone for hours, picking right up where we'd left off. She'd interrogate me.

"Any cute guys in Sac?" she'd ask, always eager to hear about my dating prospects.

"Yeah, there's a few cute guys here."

I didn't have to ask her if she had met anybody new or interesting. She'd been dating the same guy since we'd met in junior high. His name was Tyrone.

"Tyrone and I got a little place together over in Hollywood. You know I love me some Tyrone. He's so fine! We'll get married and I'll have his babies someday."

"Girl, we're too young to be thinking about marriage and having anybody's babies!"

"I know, but I'm just saying . . ."

Tyrone and Valorie really did love each other, and I admired the fact that they were so sure of their relationship despite being so young. I think they both knew that they were meant to be together from the moment they met.

The two had been introduced while hanging out with Valorie's cousins in her grandmother's garage. It had been converted into a hangout space. I teased her about meeting the love of her life in a garage, of all places.

"I hope that you're not planning to tell your future children that you met their father in a garage."

She'd cut her eyes at me when I teased her about Tyrone. It was payback for all the times she had made fun of my boyfriends over the years. It was all in good jest. I loved Tyrone like a brother.

I confided that I'd met someone, but I did my best to downplay our relationship. As expected, a barrage of questions followed: "Who is he? Where's he from? What does he look like? When will Tyrone and I get to meet him?"

"Okay, now you're asking too many questions," I told her. "It's not serious enough for me to want to have his babies yet, if that's what you're wondering."

"Well, I hope I like him better than I liked Gordy. I want you to be with someone who treats you right."

"You mean like Tyrone treats you?"

She and Tyrone were basically married already. He loved her. It was no surprise they were ready to make it legal.

I'd met Guss on the first day of the fall semester at Sac State. Well, we sort of met that day. I was taking an exercise class near the gym. Guss played basketball for the university, so he spent a lot of time in the gym, training. As I recall, I was walking down the hall minding my own business (looking fly, of course!), when this really tall guy passed me by. He smiled and paused as if he wanted to say something, but he didn't.

Awkward, I thought to myself and kept walking.

I started seeing that same guy at various places around campus. I had passed him at the library, the PE building, the Quad, but he never said anything to me or introduced himself. Now mind you, I'm an LA girl and we're a little bold. I told myself that the next time I saw him, I was going to introduce myself to him instead. Then at least we could stop having these *close encounters.*

Beautiful orange and red leaves blanketed the library lawn on that crisp fall day. As summer gave way to fall, it felt as if I were embarking on a new season in my life. Eager to meet people my age, I decided to check out the Campus Fair. Sac State had more to offer in the way of *extra curricular* activities than Dominquez Hills had.

A girl that I recognized from my Communications class handed me an invite. She was a member of the AKA's (Alpha Kappa Alpha sorority).

"I'd love for you to meet some of the other sisters. Rush week is coming and we'll be accepting new members." I didn't know much about sorority life, but I told her that I'd try to make the meeting.

I gravitated toward a table that appeared to be a book club of some sort. A young woman greeted me. Radiating warmth and hospitality, she handed me a little green book, encouraging me to immerse myself in its pages. She also invited me to an event her group was hosting.

"Sure thing," I said, realizing I now had the sorority invite and the book club to consider. My options were already looking better. Sac State was by no means a party school, but it at least had a more energetic vibe.

As I turned to leave the book club table, a young woman tapped me on the shoulder.

"Excuse me," she said. "Guss and Taps asked me to come and invite you to join us at the basketball team's Booster Club table."

"Who?" I was sure she'd mistaken me for someone else.

She repeated herself and then pointed to two guys standing at a table near the library. By the puzzled look on my face, she realized that I didn't know the guys who had sent her on a would be dating mission.

"Oh my gosh, I'm so embarrassed," she said. "My two friends sent me down here to talk to you. Maybe they're pranking me. You don't know them, do you?"

"I sure don't." I took a second look. It was the guy I'd been noticing around campus.

Well, I'm tired of this, I thought to myself. *I'm going to go meet this guy so he can stop stalking me.*

I marched myself right up the library ramp to introduce myself. "I'm Christa, and you are?"

He smiled. His approach had worked. "My name is Guss, and this is my roommate, Taps. Nice to finally meet you," he said. I smiled too. Mission accomplished. Then I turned around and left. Now that we had officially met each other, we'd stop from time to time in between classes and make small talk. One day, we struck up a conversation about how we had spent the weekend. This particular time Guss didn't have on his usual Sac State Hornets T-shirt and team-issued sweatpants. He was dressed up, which caught my attention.

We stood there after class talking longer than usual. I felt relaxed in his presence. He was easygoing and funny.

"Coach had the team over to his house for barbecue."

My eyes lit up. He was speakin' my love language! "Oh, what I wouldn't do for some good barbecue! I miss Woody's," I said. "That's my spot back home. They don't have barbecue like that here in Sac."

Guss quickly responded. "Me, Taps, and Corn," short for Cornell, "barbecue all the time at our apartment. Why don't you come over and I'll hook you up?"

In my excitement, I quickly agreed. *Free food, I'll take it.*

I really did miss Woody's Barbecue.

"Hey, wait!" he called out behind me. "I don't have your number."

Without hesitation, I gave it to him. He called me that night and solidified our plans for barbecue on that Friday.

That evening, as I got out of my car to walk up to his apartment, it suddenly dawned on me that I had agreed *to a date with Guss.* I laughed. *Naw, this isn't a date. This is just good eatin'.*

I knocked on the door of his apartment and a girl answered. *Oh, no! He has a girlfriend?* I awkwardly tried to play it off as if I had the wrong address. I didn't want to make any trouble for Guss, and it wasn't too late to politely excuse myself from this love triangle.

But before I could leave, Guss suddenly came from around the door with a big grin on his face, indicating he was happy to see me. "You're here. Come in."

Maybe I'd misread his signals. Maybe he was just a nice guy who had invited me over to hang out with his friends. Maybe it really was all about the barbecue! I sat down on the couch as he introduced me to the girl who had answered the door.

"This is Jules, my roommate's girlfriend," he explained. She greeted me and then she abruptly grabbed her purse and hurried off. Guss explained that she was upset because her boyfriend, Taps, had stood her up.

That night, Guss and I talked for hours, and I forgot all about the fact that he'd invited me over for barbecue. Turned out, there wasn't a grill in sight. He did, however, take me out for pizza.

Later, Guss's third roommate, Corn, walked in. "You're the redhead my boy has been talkin' about, huh? Nice to finally meet you." He gave Guss that "You go, boy!" look, followed by a fist pound.

"So, you've been talking about me, huh?"

Guss smiled. "Well, Corn runs his mouth too much, but yeah. I've been tellin' him about you for a while."

From that night on, Guss and I continued to hang out almost every day. He kept inviting me over, and I kept saying yes. We became inseparable around campus. I met his teammates and coaches and started regularly attending his basketball games. Guss was different from the guys I had dated in the past. It didn't seem like he had anything to prove. There was a genuineness about him. Exactly the kind of guy I needed in my life.

I eventually confessed to Valorie that I really liked him and that we were dating. She interrogated me like any best friend would.

"Slow down," I told her. "We'll see where this goes." But I already knew that things between us were getting serious.

17

LOVE &
BASKETBALL

Our romance continued to blossom. We were inseparable—a series of chance encounters had led to an undeniable connection, something neither of us had expected.

Guss left his hometown of Lompoc for Sacramento with the one-hundred-dollar bill his father had given him in his pocket and verbal commitment of a scholarship from Sac State's basketball coach, a man he'd only spoken to a few times on the phone.

"You just get here, son, and we'll take care of ya!"

In Guss's mind that meant that he had been offered a basketball scholarship. All those long hours he had spent in the gym had paid off. More importantly, he was thankful that he didn't have to join the Air Force, as so many of his friends had. There weren't a lot of options for young men like him, who had grown up in the small military community of Lompoc.

He certainly didn't want the life his father had. Too many rules and too much movin'. When Guss arrived at Sacramento State, there was no apartment or job waiting for him, and no scholarship, as the coach had promised him—but he'd already made up his mind that he wasn't going home. He was going to play ball and earn his degree, no matter what it took.

By day, Guss was an athlete on the college campus. By night, he was pushing mops, emptying trash cans, and cleaning toilets for a large insurance company in order to pay his share of the rent. The small paycheck didn't afford him a full bedroom, so a makeshift setup in the living room would have to do.

But I didn't care as much about money as I did about dating someone who'd treat me is there an extra space?with respect. That was enough for me. It didn't hurt that he had a great sense of humor.

When you're starving college students, you learn to be creative and to improvise. So, on Friday nights, he would invite me up to *his office*— AKA the building he and Corn had been hired to clean—for a *dinner date*.

"Look what I found in the fridge," Guss said as if he had struck gold. It reminded me of the time I found that shiny pink bike as a little girl. Instinctively, I knew that whatever he had discovered didn't belong to him.

There had been some sort of office party earlier that day. Guss began pulling out leftovers, and let's just say we both helped ourselves to the remaining lasagna, pasta salad, and the half-eaten cake. It had the remnants of Joe's name and a congratulatory message, wishing him the *best of luck* in his new job, inscribed on it. The romantic mood was all set when Guss shut off half the fluorescent lighting in the office break room. The only thing that was missing was a violinist.

Guss only earned minimum wage, but his janitorial job did have its perks. Free long-distance phone calls. His roommate Corn had been the one to discover the bonus benefit. Corn would do his share of cleaning and, when his shift was over, he'd spend the remainder of the evening talking to his fiancée, who lived several thousand miles away in North Carolina. They'd talk until the wee hours of the morning. Making expensive calls to Valorie and my family back home wasn't exactly in my budget, especially when the funds on my calling card were all used up. Guss invited me to come up to the offices and call home whenever I wanted or needed to. Valorie and I would sometimes talk for hours. We had a lot to catch up on.

When we weren't out on our "fancy dinner dates," we were either hanging out at his apartment—watching some silly comedy—or I was attending one of his basketball games. I was proud of *my boo*, and I wanted the whole campus to know it. I'd cheer and scream so loud, you would have thought the Hornets were the Georgetown Hoyas or some other great college team. I always sat right behind the bench with the other players' girlfriends, so that whenever one our guys would make a pretty pass or hit a jumper, we could all yell at the top of our lungs. I left most games with a sore throat, but nothing was too good for my man. One night, after a huge win against the UC Davis Aggies, Guss stepped out of the locker room looking a bit off, which was unusual, especially since we had just beaten our rivals. "I got something to tell you, but I don't want you to be upset," he said.

I should have known our relationship was too good to be true.

He paused and I braced myself for the bad news . . . that he was interested in seeing other people or that he wanted to break up altogether. I was already preparing my comeback in my head. *It's cool, I don't want to be in a serious relationship anyway.* These were lies, of course, but I didn't want to appear too needy—vulnerability was unattractive.

"Coach said you can't sit behind the bench and cheer anymore." Guss explained. "He said you're too loud and it's taking away from the game. We can't focus."

What? Here I was thinking that we were going to break up and all he wanted to tell me was that I couldn't sit behind the bench at his games anymore. The next game, I moved my seat away from the bench. Of course, that didn't stop me from being the loudest one in the gym. I never spoke of the whole breakup ordeal I had made up in my head. I wasn't ready for Guss to know about my abandonment issues.

A few weeks later, Guss called to tell me some *real* bad news. He and Corn had gotten fired from their janitorial jobs.

"What?" Had they figured out we had been raiding the lunchroom refrigerator?

"Naw," Guss said. "We got fired for making all those long distance calls home. My mom just told me they called the house in Lompoc, asking if she knew anyone who lived in Sacramento.

"What did she tell them?" I wondered if the investigators had tried to reach my aunts or Valorie? It was a rare occasion to catch Mama at home, so I wasn't at all worried about them reaching her.

We weren't trying to be criminals. We were just broke students who were staying in touch with our people. I'm not sure how we were officially busted but I guess it didn't take much investigation to figure out that it wasn't any of their actual employees who were stealing precious phone minutes, since none of them worked the night shift.

Guss and his roommates were constantly facing financial difficulties. He would sometimes tell me stories about how he would go days without eating. When money was really tight, he would sneak around the grocery store across the street from his apartment and consume an entire meal without paying for it. In his mind this wasn't technically stealing. I tried to imagine a six-foot four, young Black man, walking around the grocery store, grabbing Wonder Bread, ham, and cheese, without being noticed. Maybe someone felt sorry for him, so they turned a blind eye to the sandwich bandit. Things weren't looking so good now that they had been fired.

One month later, Guss and his roommates came home to a *Notice to Vacate* the premises! They had three days to pay or leave. So, we did the only thing that a couple who was young, broke, and in love would do at a time like that. We moved in together. Guss and I packed up what few belongings we had, said goodbye to our roommates, and found a very affordable apartment that wasn't too far from campus.

I would describe our first apartment as modest. Okay, so that was a nice way of saying we had *nothing* and it was a *dump*! We picked up our first couch from the Goodwill drop-off trailer. Someone had conveniently left it for us—or so we told ourselves. Luckily, no one caught us hauling that big orange sofa across the street and up the stairs to our love nest. I put a decorative pillow over the huge rip and called it good.

What we were lacking in the finer things, we made up for with chemistry and laughter. Everyone thought Guss was quiet, but when you got to know him, as I had, you'd learn that he wasn't quiet at all. He was actually pretty funny.

What wasn't so funny was our financial situation. Turns out our affordable apartment was worse than we thought. Unbeknownst to us, we had landed ourselves right in the middle of some sort of crime ring. Coming from the 'hood myself, I'm surprised I hadn't noticed sooner that we were in danger. Under normal circumstances, my

Spidey senses would have kicked in immediately. I guess the saying is true— "Love is blind." Being in love with Guss had definitely softened me.

One morning we were leaving the apartment, heading to class, when we heard voices coming from right beneath our balcony. I assumed it was our downstairs neighbor. We hadn't seen much of him in several weeks. As we were exiting our apartment, we noticed a group of people wearing what looked to me like military tactical gear. They had surrounded the downstairs neighbor's apartment. We decided that whoever this group of people were, it wasn't safe to leave, so we retreated back inside.

Later that afternoon, one of our other neighbors explained what had gone down earlier that morning.

"SWAT swooped in today and arrested the guy downstairs and everyone in his apartment. They were all handcuffed and taken away in a police van." Apparently my neighbor was involved in a major drug ring. We had no idea that we were living right among methamphetamine dealers. I thought I had left that all behind me when I left The Jungle.

I couldn't help but think about the time that I had been naive enough to smuggle a dime bag of weed into the girls' bathroom. Thankfully, Gordy had been a small-time drug dealer, or my fate could have been different. I wondered if he had continued in his life of crime or worse—was he even still alive? I was thankful to have escaped that life.

The trajectory of my future had changed by going to college. Sac State felt like another planet compared to growing up in The Jungle. Being in a relationship with Guss felt entirely different from the relationships I was accustomed to. Guss was simple. He had never even had a drink before. His decision not to drink had been based on watching a close family member struggle with addiction for years.

"I never wanted to be drunk or high, all I want to do is to play ball. That's my addiction," he said matter-of-factly.

I never told him about the time close relatives had allowed me to drink and to get high with them. I also never told him about my drug dealing days. I didn't want him to run.

18

CHANGE IS GOING TO COME

As I reflect on my childhood and adolescent years, I realize that though I was never officially diagnosed with PTSD, the profound experiences and the emotional turmoil that I endured had a lasting psychological effect on me. Anyone who grows up with persistent trauma, shame, and dysfunction, like I did, undoubtedly fits the profile of someone who suffers from post-traumatic stress disorder.

Growing up in the Nation of Islam, during those crucial developmental years of my life, had a significant negative impact on me. Years later, I was still feeling the after-effects of the Nation's indoctrination. The message that the White man was the devil was drilled into my head so much that it almost became my truth. The danger of believing that ideology was that if it were true, then that meant that at least half of me was evil too. I wanted to distance myself from anything that reminded me of being White or evil.

Even after we left the Nation of Islam, my struggles with identity and the challenges of being biracial continued to linger. To clear up any confusion about my identity, I sunbathed religiously… year-round in fact. That was the only way I could keep my skin brown; otherwise, I was pale, just like my father. Tanning wasn't merely a leisurely activity for me, it held a profound personal significance— it was a means to reconcile my identity.

Sometimes I'd tan so long that I'd end up with a horrendous case of sunburn—my skin would burn so badly that I would peel down to the pink layer. But even that didn't deter me from tanning incessantly. I was willing to endure almost any discomfort in order to achieve the thing that was most important to me—being identified as Black. All my life, I had been asked the same question— "What are you?" Being constantly questioned about my ethnicity was one more assault on my identity and self worth.

I was tired of being the unicorn. I was tired of feeling like the *only one*! The only one in my neighborhood who was biracial. The only one who had freckles and red hair, and the only one who secretly had a father who was a Catholic priest. I imagined that explaining my uniqueness would have been less complicated if my father had stuck around and married my mother. At least then I'd be able to explain that I looked like him. But he hadn't given me that option.

I can still remember the time that I had my first real makeover. I didn't wear much makeup in high school, but I wanted to look my best for my senior portraits. I was so proud of the fact that I had been able to save enough money to be able to afford a real makeover, done by a professional. So I booked an appointment at a cosmetic counter at my favorite mall, the Beverly Center.

Almost immediately, the woman at the counter seemed a little flustered. She had gone through several applications and shades of foundation, trying to find just the right match to complement my complexion.

"Let's see . . . no . . . that shade has too much pink in it, you have golden undertones," she said, mumbling under her breath. "Finally," she said. "I think I have a good match."

I abruptly interrupted her, ruining her victorious moment.

"That's not the correct shade at all, not even close!" I mused over the other foundation samples that had a darker hue, finally selecting the shade I believed to be mine. "Can we try this one?"

Before she could respond, I applied a small dab to my face and attempted to blend it in, as I had seen her do. Despite my best efforts, the foundation I had chosen for myself wasn't blending at all, it was too dark for my complexion. There was a clear line of demarcation, separating my face from my neck. In my denial, I was unfazed by it.

The fact that something as tangential as skin color would be a tool by which we measure a person's worth is difficult to comprehend, especially when you are a kid. It would be several years before I could fully begin to unpack just how deeply my identity had been shaped by the lens of others. During my therapy sessions with Cathy, we had gone deep enough to talk about my issues with my father, but I had built a protective wall around my most vulnerable self, that even she couldn't cross over. It would be a few years before I would be brave enough to confront the distorted views I held of myself. The path toward self-acceptance would be marked by many starts and stops along the way.

***

As was my routine, I was poolside obtaining a golden-brown glow when a tall, slender man approached me.

"Hey there!" The man drawled. "I hope I'm not interrupting you."

Actually, you are, was the response that was right on the tip of my tongue—but I let it stay there.

"Where are my manners? I'm James, your next-door neighbor. My wife Gladys and I live just on the other side of you. I met your husband Guss last week and I thought I'd come over and introduce myself to you. He said that you liked hanging out at the pool. I knew it was you because of the red hair."

I guess Guss had told him that I had red hair and that I could be found sun worshipping by the pool. But I'm sure Guss hadn't told him we were married—we just lived together.

"I dropped off some of my wife's sweet potato pie to Guss. You better make sure you get some."

I only had a half hour to catch some good rays, but the man kept going on and on about those pies.

"I'm sure you ain't never had sweet potato pie this good before. My wife put her foot in this batch. Her pies are good, but when she's making them for the Lord, they are even more divine."

Now, I was a bit confused. How do you make pie for the Lord? I began packing up my sun tanning essentials to head back to our place. I was hoping Guss had saved me a taste of this so-called heavenly pie.

As I was leaving, James stopped me. "If you enjoy the pie, wait until you taste some of her other specialties. We would love to have the two of you over for dinner sometime. That way Guss and I can talk basketball. Believe it or not, I was pretty good at hoops back in my day."

James was tall and skinny, but he didn't look like he was any good at playing basketball.

Just as promised, we were invited over a few weeks later.

Gladys and James were as southern as it gets, and they still had the southern accents to prove it. That night at dinner, James not only bragged about his wife's cooking, but he also bragged about her singing.

My ears perked up.

"Gladys is what you call a songbird. I knew I wanted to marry her the first time I heard her sing. After I tasted her cooking, I ran out and bought a ring."

I couldn't tell if he was joking or not.

I had never heard the term *songbird* before, but I figured it had something to do with her being from Texas.

During dinner, as Gladys passed me the macaroni and cheese and candied yams, she sweetly asked, "Do y'all go to church?"

I wasn't much of a churchgoer. Guss and I had visited St. John's Baptist Church once, but we hadn't been back. His dad knew the pastor there and had basically volun*told* Guss that he should attend. Guss had grown up going to church, but I guess you could say he was taking a break from religion.

I could count on one hand the number of times I'd ever been to church. One Easter, I went to church with my great-grandmother, Mamo. They were having an Easter egg hunt. I remember wearing a pretty, pale-blue dress, ruffled white socks—the kind with the lace around the ankles—and a daisy bonnet. We didn't get dressed up very often, but when you go to church, it's like attending a wedding or something—it's the time when you pull out your best.

Before either of us could respond, Gladys said, "Y'all should come visit us at our church. Bethel."

In between bites of cornbread and yams, I responded. "Sure, we'll come. Sounds fun."

That Easter had certainly been memorable. I hoped to enjoy my neighbors' church as much as I had enjoyed spending that Easter with Mamo. Besides, I couldn't have said no to Gladys—especially after she'd fed us all that delicious food. That night, we ate so much that my stomach hurt. I was stuffed. *Maybe they'll invite us over for dinner again after church,* I thought to myself. I hadn't eaten this good in awhile. Gladys' cooking made me miss Valorie, Mama Shirley, and those weekends I would spend with their family.

One Saturday, Guss and I were about to tackle our typical weekend ritual of washing our clothes before a trip to the movies. I thought about our dinner with the neighbors and about their invitation to go to church. Guss had just come back from working out. I greeted him with a kiss and leaned in close to him. "What do you think about going to church tomorrow?"

"It's been a while. I guess that would be cool. I'll call James and see what time the Service starts?"

James offered us a ride and told us to be ready by nine. I picked out the most appropriate outfit I could find in my closet. I didn't own a dress, but I did have a cute pink mini skirt ensemble. It was my go to outfit for any special event. A team dinner, the club, and now church. *This should do.* I thought I looked presentable enough.

Guss and his teammates were accustomed to dressing up for team booster events and an occasional award ceremony, for which he hoped to be nominated as the point guard of the year. But he'd have to settle on being the best free throw shooter on the team. Guss pulled the nicest pair of slacks he owned from the back of the closet and topped them with an argyle sweater. The preppy look, as we called it, was popular in the 80s.

James blew the horn for us at nine a.m. sharp. We hopped into their station wagon and headed for church. Guss and James talked about basketball the whole way there. While I tried to build up the courage to ask Gladys to teach me how to make her mac and cheese, James and Guss bantered back and forth about who the best player in the NBA was. James was a huge Houston Rockets fan, so he argued that Hakeem Olajuwon was the best player. Guss was a Lakers fan. Hands down, Magic Johnson deserved the honors, in his opinion.

Bethel was located right in the heart of the urban hub of Sacramento's famed Oak Park neighborhood. Oak Park had once been a pristine, upper-class community that boasted of prominent businesses and land-wealthy residents, but things had drastically changed. The community had been in decline for several years.

On our way into the area, I noticed that several "working girls" were out that morning in hopes of capturing a few early rising customers. It was easy to identify them by their "work uniforms." They were wearing just the right amount of clothing to attract business, but not to be arrested for indecent exposure.

At first glance, many of these women looked too old to be in this line of work, but up close, you could tell that most of them weren't old at all. Street life, drugs, poverty, and abuse of every kind imaginable, had not only robbed them of their innocence and dignity, but it had also stolen their youthfulness.

As we turned into the parking lot, one of the women approached the station wagon, as if she were all ready to set up shop right there in front of us. I'm not sure if James had given her a stern look, or if seeing other women in the car was a deterrent, but the young woman quickly turned in the other direction—sashaying her way down Broadway, half naked, as if all was normal.

As we made our way from the car to the church, I tried to forget the image I had just seen. I put the woman and her business out of my mind and focused on the people inside instead. An usher greeted us at the door, handing each of us a fan with an advertisement for the local funeral home on back that read, "Our day begins when yours ends." *I hope I don't need their services anytime soon!*

I looked around and noticed that several of the ladies had worn the most beautiful hats, all perfectly coordinated with their pearls and Sunday suits. I felt underdressed, but I decided I wouldn't let that stop me from enjoying our outing. I had really come to hear Gladys sing. We could have skipped everything else and moved straight to the musical part.

I'm not sure what I was expecting, but the church was much smaller than I had imagined. I immediately noticed that there were no beautiful stained-glass windows or lavish furnishings. The wooden pews were a little dated. Faux wood paneling covered the walls as far as the eye could see, which wasn't very far. A picture of an older man, clutching a very large gold encrusted Bible, hung on the wall, along with a placard noting last weekend's attendance and offering. There had been a total of fifty-two people in attendance the week prior and they raised a whopping $252.39. I guess some of the children had tossed in a few coins, accounting for the thirty-nine cents.

Guss and I sat down on a freshly polished pew, which made it easier to slide over as the late arrivals joined our row. I scanned the room. If the walls could talk, I imagined they would tell the stories of the generations of people who had previously gathered at this very same place to meet with God. Their effects had left a tangible residue. That feeling that makes the hair on your arms stand up. It was almost electric. I had never experienced anything quite like it before.

As the service began, an elderly woman stood up and began talking. I thought sure she might be out of order, but no one said anything to her, so I assumed her sudden outburst was something people were accustomed to. "I want to thank the Lord this morning for His goodness to me down through the years. He's been so faithful. He's been good. Hallelujah!"

The rest of the congregation responded in kind.

"Um-hum!"

"He's sho 'nuff been good," another sister said in agreement.

I sat wide eyed and took it all in. Before I knew it, I was nodding my head too as if I had been present for some of this goodness myself.

"Amen, sister!" others proclaimed in tandem.

"Our God has been good."

"He's good all the time!"

Being in church was inspiring. I wondered why I hadn't gone more often. Maybe subconsciously, my father had something to do with that.

Finally, I caught a glimpse of Gladys as she approached the front of the church where an old B3 Hammond organ sat. The room grew quiet. The pastor sat in his chair with his eyes closed and his hands folded, as if he was in deep thought. Anticipation filled the atmosphere. I waited along with the others, wondering what would happen next.

A melodious sound began to overtake the room.

"All to Jesus I surrender, all to Him I freely give," Gladys sang, filling the entire church with her angelic voice. "I surrender all. All to thee, my blessed Savior, I surrender all."

In that moment, I learned what a songbird was.

A songbird was a spirited Gospel singer whose words and voice spoke to you and tugged at your soul, as if you were the only person in the room.

I hadn't noticed that my eyes had become a little misty. I quickly patted away my tears on the sleeve of my jacket and hoped no one had seen me crying. James was right! Gladys was a beautiful singer. Her music was different from the music I had grown up listening to. The songs I loved singing were mostly about the relationships between men and women. Gladys was singing about God. *What does she mean by surrendering all to Him? How do you do that?*

She sang and played that morning like she was someone else, not the sweet southern belle who'd graciously welcomed us into her home for dinner. There was something very moving about the words she sang. She continued, "Let me feel thy Holy Spirit, Truly knowing that Thou art mine."

After Gladys's powerful performance, the pastor got up and spoke. I tried to relate my life to the Bible passage he had chosen to share on that morning. He told a story about a time Jesus had gone out of His way to meet a woman, who was from a place that I had never heard of before—Samaria. Her story caught my attention. She had been labeled as a social outcast, because of her mixed ethnicity. She had a bad reputation because she had been married five times.

From the pastor's message that morning, I gathered that this woman knew something about pain and rejection. She was looked down upon in her community. From what I could understand of her story, it seemed as if she was being shunned for being unlucky in love. A successful marriage eluded her. Perhaps the reason she had been married five times was because she was afraid to be alone. Or, just maybe, the men in her life had abandoned her for their own frivolous reasons. I was deeply troubled by the fact that this woman seemed to carry so much shame and blame. The story hit too close to home. Mama had been forced to wear a scarlet letter—U. *Unwed!* While my father was allowed to stay in the priesthood, and to go on about his life with seemingly no consequences. And the church did nothing about it either.

But it seemed as if Jesus really saw this woman and that He valued her in spite of how others felt.

I thought about speaking to the pastor after church was over. Maybe he'd be able to shed some light on things for me. What had

Jesus meant when He promised to give her living water? What kind of water could permanently quench her thirst? I was intrigued. I had heard that Jesus worked a few miracles in His day. Was this another one of those miracles? Did the story have a deeper meaning I wasn't aware of?

Toward the end of his message, the pastor began explaining . . .

"The woman had come to the well because she had a physical need. Jesus had intentionally taken a detour through her city that day, just to meet her— He's still going out of the way today. He's offering healing and new life."

I knew all too well that emotional scars were the worst kind of wounds we humans can have. They are more complex and take longer to heal. I began to think about the woman we had the close encounter with in the parking lot, earlier that morning. She certainly seemed like she could benefit from some encouragement in her life. I wondered if the pastor had ever considered taking his *positive message to the streets?*

My heart went out to her. At one point in time, my own mother found herself in similar circumstances. Thankfully, several people had been willing to lend a hand along the way.

The pastor stepped down from the platform and got closer to us. It was almost too close, but I was willing to overlook being uncomfortable, because the story was so compelling. I hung on every word.

"After the woman at the well met Jesus, her whole life changed. She ran back to her town and told them all about her encounter with the Rabbi. 'You have to come and see this man,' she said. 'He knew all about me even though we had never met before. I think this is the one our great grandparents told us about.' That same day, many people followed the woman to hear Jesus' teaching for themselves. I guess they had forgotten all about her soiled reputation. Whatever it was that Jesus had offered this woman seemed to be working. His impact on her life had been profound."

The pastor continued. "Some of you here this morning can relate to the Samaritan woman. You know what it's like to feel desperate. In a moment, I'd like to pray with you." He paused, as if he was getting a message, telepathically. "God is speaking to you. Just like sister Gladys sang, it's time to surrender your life to Him."

I looked around the room, wondering who the person was that God was speaking to. Perhaps his message was for one of the congregants who had spoken earlier that morning about God being good and all. No one moved. I was beginning to feel badly for the pastor. It appeared as if he might have had a bad connection with whoever it was he was receiving his promptings from.

"You know what it's like to be rejected by people." He continued. "You've often felt alone and unloved."

And with that, I was no longer thinking about the woman we'd encountered in the parking lot that morning or the other people at the church—his words were now touching my heart. Growing up without a father—one who was supposed to be a representative of God, for that matter, cut deep. Bearing the burden of my own mother's emotional trauma almost destroyed me. It was the reason I'd attempted to take my own life as a teen.

I tuned back in.

"Surrendering yourself to God is the single most important decision you'll ever make in your life. Jesus surrendered His life on the cross so that you could have a relationship with God the Father."

I had never heard of God being described as a father. *A relationship with my father is what I had longed for my entire life.* Was it really possible for God to love me in a way that my father hadn't?

I had some doubt, but I was willing to try. I had tried everything else. The God thing worked for the woman at the well and seemed to be working for James and Gladys. Perhaps there was hope for me.

Now I was certain that the person the pastor had been speaking about all along was actually me. I needed a relationship with this Father.

For years, I had been looking to be loved and approved of. Time and time again, I had been disappointed. I was certainly disappointed at that first meeting with my father, sitting across from him at what felt to me like a board meeting instead of a homecoming.

I had found my father, but I hadn't found his love.

But, there in church, the most beautiful thing happened. A feeling of love and acceptance began to wash over me. Was this what the woman experienced when she met Jesus on that afternoon?

Suddenly, I felt as if I were being drawn forward. For a fleeting moment, I thought about Guss. *Was he feeling what I was feeling?* The thought left my mind almost as quickly as it had come. I stood up and made my way to the front of the room, where the pastor was standing. He spoke to me, looking directly at me as if he knew me.

"God led you here today," he said. "It's okay to let go! You can lay all your troubles at His feet. The Father loves you."

The part about the Father's love *broke me!* Tears began to stream down my face, only this time, I didn't try to wipe them away. The floodgates had opened and there was no damming them up now.

I was happy to lay it all down. I was tired of carrying around the heavy weight of secrecy and the shame of being the unwanted, *illegitimate* daughter of a Catholic priest. I wanted to lay down the burden of the broken relationship between my mother and myself. If God could help with all of that, then I was in.

By that time, I was crying the ugly cry, snot and all. I sobbed and repeated the pastor's words. *God if You can, please heal my heart.*

The pastor's words assured me. "When you give your life to God, it's like starting all over again—you become a new person."

I welcomed this new beginning.

It was as if a huge weight was being lifted off my shoulders. I glanced over at Gladys, who was also crying tears of joy. The whole church seemed to be happy for me. Even the children came forward to congratulate me. It was a sweet moment.

I caught a glimpse of James—who was smiling from ear to ear.

He went up to Guss and began to shake his hand profusely. "Congratulations, brother."

It had been such a personal, one-on-one moment between God and me that I hadn't noticed that Guss had come forward to give his life to God alongside me. Had it been Gladys's song or the pastor's words that had moved him to come forward?

Either way, I was glad that we would be embarking on this new journey together.

19

THE CLASSROOM

I don't think James and Gladys expected us to make such a big commitment on our very first visit to Bethel. We hadn't either! The kind couple continued to endow us with their southern hospitality. I still loved it when James would bring over a piece or two of Gladys's sweet potato pie. I enjoyed the conversations she and I would have about her own personal faith journey. We would sometimes talk for hours. I had so many unanswered questions. Like, why a loving God allowed bad things to happen to innocent people?

I had grown up hearing a lot of second hand information about God. But hearing about God and knowing if what you've learned of Him is true, was something altogether different. My experience on spiritual matters was limited. Most of what I had learned had to do with rules. *No drinking, no smoking, and no sex.* Of course my father had convinced my mother that the latter didn't apply—at least to them.

I was grappling with my father's failings, and I was still angry with the Catholic Church for their refusal to protect people like my mother and me. For years, church officials had been complicit in perpetuating sexual abuse by covering it up. They had hidden behind the "secrecy" rule in cases of child sexual abuse, enabling the widespread abuse to continue. Instead of protecting the victims, they protected the abusers. It was going to take time to sort all of this out but one thing was clear to me, God was not responsible for the failures of the church nor of my father.

Over the next several months, I did what Mama had always encouraged me to do—

Learn. I became a student in the classroom of faith. I carefully studied the people at Bethel and the Book that they promised had the power to transform lives. Sharing testimonies was a regular part of the church service. People would tell miraculous stories of how they had been changed and of how God had brought them through difficulty. Testimony Service was one of the best parts of my Sunday. Hearing these stories inspired and encouraged me. Some of the people at Bethel had overcome extraordinary circumstances. I was thankful to have discovered God's love.

The people at Bethel continued to welcome us in. It was obvious that they wanted to make sure we'd keep coming back. The young pastor, his wife Gloria, and their three children had been assigned to Bethel to breathe new life into the congregation. They were certainly breathing new life into Guss and me. They took us under their wings and began to unofficially mentor us.

For them, being a Christian meant living a life of generosity and hospitality. They won us over by inviting us to spend time with their family. In tangible and practical ways, they were helping us to understand the nature and character of God. They made a relationship with Him seem attainable and personal.

"Spiritual growth is a matter of spending intentional time in community with others, reading and praying," they would say.

"God will speak to you, if you're willing to make time to listen," Gloria reminded me of this often.

At first, this confused me. *Does she mean that God was going to speak to me in an audible voice?* I was nervous about the whole prayer thing, but I had a deep respect for Gloria, so I heeded her advice.

Just as she promised, prayer, coupled with the Tuesday evening Bible studies, were definitely instrumental in helping Guss and me understand God in a way we hadn't before.

One morning, I decided to put Gloria's advice to go deeper into practice: "Find yourself a quiet spot in your apartment, where you won't be distracted, to pray and talk with God uninterrupted."

The only quiet, private spot in our small studio apartment was an even tinier bathroom, but it would have to do.

I closed the door and knelt beside the tub. "God, I'm, uh, new to this listening-to-You thing. How will I really know if it's You speaking to me or if it's my own voice I'm hearing? Uh, where do I begin?"

Silence.

My mind drifted off for a little bit. Five minutes felt like an hour.

It was awkward at first, but I kept going back for those intimate meetings with God. It took a while, but eventually I began to recognize God's voice from my own. His voice wasn't condemning or judgmental. It was loving and affirming. I was much harder on myself than God was. Negative self-talk was a common practice of mine. A bad habit I found difficult to break. It was hard to silence the inner voice in my head that constantly told me that I wasn't enough.

In Bible study, I was being introduced to different passages that began to refute the negative things I had believed about myself for years. There was one passage in particular that I had been wrestling with for several months. It described the conception of human beings as a "marvelous act of God," and it went on to say that we had "been beautifully created" by Him. These were difficult words to accept. From my vantage point, there was nothing marvelous or beautiful about my birth. There was a lot of damage that needed undoing, but being in community with other people who were willing to walk with me through my struggles was transformative.

I was building a new, healthy life in Sacramento, falling deeper in love with Guss, pursuing my college education, and learning what it meant to trust God in new ways. But my old life wasn't ready to let me go quite yet.

My mother had finally found the courage to speak out against the Catholic Church and give voice to the abuse she'd endured as a teenager. By nothing short of another miracle, she had somehow managed to get Gloria Allred, the tenacious legal genius, to take her case.

"Gloria believed me," my mother said, relieved that she was finally being heard after all those years.

The next time I would lock eyes with my father would be in a lawyer's office. He wasn't going to give in without a fight. The courts ordered us to take a paternity test. I couldn't believe it. *Is he actually contesting the fact that he is my father?* He'd sat across that table and seen how much I looked like; I had his dimpled chin, his large ears, and his red hair. All those old feelings resurfaced.

My mother was outraged. "As if I was sleeping around with another man? I was in love with your father and your father *only!*"

DNA testing was in its infancy in the '80s. Today, you swab your mouth, mail in the specimen to 23andMe, and await the results in the privacy of your own home. But my situation wasn't so private. The secret I had carried all my life was no longer going to be a secret.

The whole world was going to know the truth. Or at least it felt that way.

After several months of waiting, Gloria Allred's assistant called us to let us know that the paternity test results had come back and that she would be booking a flight for me to return to Los Angeles to learn the results. I'm not sure how she had done it, but somehow Mama had managed to garner the ear of one of the most powerful civil rights attorneys there was. Gloria was a champion for women—a fearless advocate for justice and equality. She was a crusader for those who had been victimized by systems of power and she wasn't afraid to call out the sins of one of the most powerful institutions that exists to this day—the Catholic Church. Mama finally had someone to help her. Someone who not only listened to her story, but believed it, and was willing to take on Goliath to prove it.

Gloria greeted us. Her firm handshake, larger-than-life confidence, and wide smile had a way of overpowering most rooms, making you forget that she only stood five foot two inches tall with heels on, I might add.

"Diane, I've got some good news for you. We now have proof that John Christenson is Christa's father. We're going to nail the bastard who ruined your lives!"

My mother sat stoic and unmoved. She hadn't needed any paternity test to prove what she had known all along.

"We have to go public with your story, Diane," Gloria said convincingly.

Although I don't think my mother needed much convincing. She had waited for a lifetime to tell her story—*our* story. Finally, people would know how her dreams had been derailed and her life had almost been completely destroyed by Father Chris.

I had only told a few close friends that we'd been invited to New York as guests on *The Phil Donahue Show*. A story like ours was almost unheard of. At that time, people weren't talking about the abuses that were going on in the Catholic Church, especially not on a nationally syndicated television show.

Gloria, Mama, and I boarded a plane headed for New York. It was only the second time I had been out of California. The first time had been when Norman, Hasan, and I traveled to Alabama.

Gloria seemed eager to introduce us to some of the finer things that people like us weren't privileged to enjoy. We took a walk through Central Park, where I saw real live carriage rides for the first time... like the ones you read about in Cinderella's fairytale. We ate at the famous restaurant, Tavern on the Green, and Mama acted like she had been there before. Our hotel room was nothing like motels I had stayed in. I discovered that rich people get little chocolates left for them on their beds and that someone comes in and turns the sheets down for them.

That next morning, my nerves got the best of me as we drove to the studio, and I began to break out in hives. Still, the show would go on.

At the studio, Gloria, Mama, and I were greeted by the show's producers and quickly whisked backstage where we were prepped for some of the questions Mr. Donahue might ask. A makeup artist came in and powdered our faces. One of the show's assistants politely pointed out to us where the restrooms were located.

"We'll be back to get you guys soon," she said as she quickly fluttered off. "Just sit tight and make yourselves comfortable."

I'm not sure how comfortable I can make myself, knowing we're about to spill our guts before thousands of people across the country. It was one thing for our story to be featured in the *Los Angeles Times*, but television was a whole different matter. Our well-kept family secret wasn't going to be so well kept anymore.

As the airtime drew near, I shifted into full fight-or-flight mode. Everything in me was telling me to *run!*

It was too late to back out. Mr. Donahue's assistant came in to get Mama and me. We were ushered onto the stage and seated in a row with several other women. They were there to tell their heartbreaking stories of being sexually abused in the church. That half an hour on live television flew by, and the audience's somber mood could clearly be felt the entire time. I don't remember much applause when the program ended. Most people sat there shocked, unsure of how to react. Mr. Donahue thanked us, and that was that. Little did I know that more than 300,000 people would hear our story that day.

A few months later, I was back in Sacramento trying to focus on my future, when the show's producers forwarded me a letter. A man who'd seen the show had taken the time to write me. He thanked me for being brave and vulnerable enough to share my story. His mother had also been in a relationship with a high-ranking clergyman, who happened to be married. In his letter he shared his heart-wrenching story of longing to know his father. I could feel the pain of his father's rejection through his letter. He had grown up living a few short miles from his father, but secrecy had kept them from ever being able to build a relationship.

I wasn't the *only one,* as I had grown up believing. Thanks to this letter, I now knew that there were others out there who had stories similar to mine. *I wasn't alone.* I was beginning to understand why Mama may have made the right choice by making her story known.

Perhaps some greater good could come out of this after all!

20

THE "M" WORD

Guss and I went from being non-church-attendees to every Sunday pewees. Bethel was small enough that everyone could technically be a part of the inner circle. If you missed a Sunday, you could expect a call from one of the members.

We were the youngest parishioners at the church, excluding the pastor's children. The Hunts embraced the idea that church was a family business. Each one of their children was to play a part in helping to further the mission. I guess you could say they were like the royal family, only with a much smaller kingdom. Each of them seemed to accept their roles and all the responsibilities that came along with it. Their oldest daughter, Stephanie, was a goal oriented perfectionist. At fourteen, she was not only the church secretary but she directed the choir and taught Sunday school. Wherever there were holes, and there were plenty of them, she'd step in.

Staci, the middle child, was independent and outspoken and prided herself on being unique. I admired how comfortable she was in her own skin. Billy, their only son, was the church drummer. He was also a basketball player. He and Guss hit it off almost immediately, bonding over sports. Billy secretly wanted to play football, but anything that required your attention or focus on Sundays was banned in the Hunt household. That included football.

Sunday was "the Lord's Day." Just in case any of his children had come down with a case of amnesia, Pastor Hunt would remind them, "We don't do anything on Sundays—it's a day that's completely dedicated to God." The Hunts took church stuff seriously. The day started at 8:00 a.m. with prayer, which was followed by Sunday School. Afterward they moved into the Morning Worship Service. They'd take a break for a few hours and come back later that night for Bible study and another evening service. There wasn't time to do anything else on Sundays, even if it had been permissible.

One weekend, I accompanied Guss on a basketball tournament. It was in Chico, California, so we missed church. That next Sunday when we returned, Pastor Hunt made a beeline for us directly after the service let out. After we caught him up on the latest happenings in our lives, he politely asked if he could set up a time to meet with us. I couldn't help but wonder if the pastor's sudden meeting request had been prompted because of our absence that previous Sunday.

"How about next Wednesday evening?" he asked.

"That should work," I said. "I don't think Guss has practice or anything."

I gave Pastor Hunt our home address.

I should have been more nervous about the fact that the pastor was requesting a personal meeting with the two of us. But I was green when it came to these matters. Guss didn't seem too enthusiastic about the meeting with Pastor Hunt.

When we got back to the apartment, I asked Guss what he thought. He was more experienced with church than I was, so he knew that a personal home visit was a *big deal*. I dug a little deeper. *Was he embarrassed by our apartment?* It was definitely the meeting's location that was troubling him, but it wasn't the modest furnishing he was concerned about. We were living together and we weren't married. Guss had concealed the fact that our living arrangement was less than ideal for respectable church folks.

His sister, Regina, had lectured him a few times over the phone. "You know Mom and Dad didn't raise us like this."

His parents had been married for over thirty five years.

"You shouldn't be living with your girlfriend. It's disrespectful to the values they have instilled in us. Besides, you know how church folks in our small town like to gossip?" In her mind, we were tarnishing the family's reputation. I knew what it was like to have a stained reputation.

Guss and I cleaned up our little place and I made it look as nice as I could. I imagined this was how my grandmother might have felt when she welcomed my father into her home. We wanted to make a good first impression. I hoped Pastor Hunt wasn't coming over to do any personal confessionals with us. It would be a long evening if that were the case.

We invited the minister into our humble apartment, and the three of us sat down at our dining room table.

"I wanted to stop by and talk to you— to see how things are going? You seem to be adjusting well."

I hadn't learned my lesson. "We love it!" I blurted out, as if I were giving answers on a game show.

Guss was smart enough to limit his conversation. A skill I had yet to acquire.

"It's good to hear that. Gloria and I have been happy to have you. And our kids . . . well, I'm sure you know how they feel about you. The two of you seemed to have been led right to our church doorstep, by God's divine plan."

I hadn't thought of it quite like that before. I believed we were there because Gladys and James had invited us. Perhaps our being there wasn't coincidental.

"Gloria and I were just a few years older than you are now when *we* got married. Shortly after our nuptials, we were called into the ministry."

Wait . . . he just mentioned the "M" word? I thought he was coming over to talk to us about missing a few too many church services. I guess Guss's sister was right after all.

"Gloria and I were talking about how much you and Guss remind us of ourselves when we were your age. We've been praying for you ever since you joined the church."

I had been doing some praying myself, just like Gloria had advised.

"The Tuesday night Bible studies have been really helpful," I said.

They had served to debunk some of the misconceptions I had about God. I believed that I had to get my life together first, before coming to Him. I imagined Him to be distant and angry. There was disconnect between who I thought God was and who He actually is. He was unimaginably kind, compassionate, and loving. His love wasn't based on my performance. The enormity of God's grace left me in awe.

I was also learning things about Jesus that I never knew. He had been sent by God the Father to love, save, and heal people, not to condemn them. He spent the majority of His life walking among the people others went out of the way to avoid—people like me, who were profoundly flawed. Jesus was brokenhearted over the conditions of our lives.

He wasn't afraid to deal with people with mental illness or physical limitations. He was a friend to the poor, the outcast, and the disenfranchised. The people Jesus seemed most comfortable to be around, and the places He frequented, reminded me of my own family and neighborhood. Jesus did His best work among those who were considered to be the "least of these." He was a champion for the underdog. He displayed His miraculous power in the lives of the people who needed it most.

In the short time I'd been attending church, I'd learned that the Bible was filled with stories of grace and redemption. If Jesus could love the characters I was reading about—then there was hope for me.

I was grateful for those who had taken the time to plant seeds of hope in my life. There was my friend Antoine from high school, who I sang with at graduation. I believe that he would be proud of me for going to church and for singing in the choir. There was also the young woman at the college fair, who had given me my very first Bible. I wished I could thank them both.

Things felt right. I was happy in my new surroundings.

"The Holy Spirit is at work in your lives," Pastor Hunt shared. "But there's room for more."

He leaned in, looking at the two of us very intently, yet tenderly. "I have to ask you a question—have you thought about the possibility of marriage?"

Marriage? That's a huge step. No one in my family had been successful in their marriages so it was hard for me to conceptualize being in that type of relationship.

This time I let Guss speak first.

"Uh . . . yes, sir. I've thought about it from our first date," Guss said.

This was news to me!

"It seems like the two of you really love each other," turning his focus to Guss, "and you've already begun to build a life together—why not consider marriage?"

I could tell that Guss was really weighing the things Pastor Hunt shared with us.

Silently, I was too.

No one had ever explained the blessings of marriage before.

"Why don't we pray about it?" Pastor Hunt grabbed both of our hands and began to pray out loud. "I ask that You would guide Guss and Christa. Give them the courage to follow You, wherever and however You might lead them. Amen!"

If I was ever going to marry anyone, it would be Guss. From the moment we'd started dating, I felt like I could trust him. If we were considering spending the rest of our lives together, nothing would matter more than trust.

I waited for Guss to take the lead. A few weeks later, he approached me. "I think we should do it," he said. "What do you think?"

"Do what?" I asked, pretending not to know what he was talking about.

"Get married."

This was a pivotal moment. Make no mistake, deciding to get married when we were only twenty and twenty-four years of age was a giant step of faith for both of us. Perhaps it was even a little foolish on our parts. But we had prayed about it, and we both felt confident that we were making the right choice.

"Let's do it," I said.

Guss called Pastor Hunt to set the date. We really wanted God's blessing on our lives and especially our relationship.

On January 30, 1987, we went down to the Sac County
Courthouse and applied for a marriage license so we could make it
official. Pastor Hunt and his wife met us at Bethel. A mutual friend
named Cathy J. served as our witness. Ironically, this was the same
spot where we'd stood just a few months prior when we made the
commitment to learn more about faith with God.

We were excited but also nervous. As we stood at the altar, it
was hard for me to believe that I was actually going to be married.
A wedding definitely hadn't been on my radar when I'd moved to
Sacramento. I'd planned to earn my degree and return home to Los
Angeles. If someone had told me that I'd be going to church twice
a week and marrying someone I'd met on campus, I wouldn't have
believed them. I had no idea that God had a plan for my life that
included marrying the tall slender basketball player, who had falsified
his barbecuing skills so that I would go out on a date with him.

Pastor Hunt was beaming with the pride of a father. I closed my
eyes for just a moment and imagined how things would have looked
differently if my father had chosen to be a part of my life. He'd be the
one to walk me down the aisle and to give me away to Guss.

"Repeat these words after me," Pastor Hunt said. "To have and
to hold, in sickness and in health, until death do us part . . ."

And within a few minutes, I became Christa Armstead. Now
that was going to take some getting used to.

Almost a year to the day later, Valorie and Tyrone got married.
I was her maid of honor. They visited with us a few times and really
seemed to like Sacramento. As expected, our Bethel family loved on
them too. On one of their visits, we talked about the possibility of
them moving to Sacramento. We even drove around looking at model
homes. I didn't think she would actually leave Mama Shirley, but I
planted the seed anyway.

21

FORGIVENESS

As I continued to grow and to heal, spending time with God became an integral part of my daily routine. For me it was like spending time with a close friend. I was a lot less patient and more prone to use certain expletives on the days that I missed my appointment with Him.

I had also grown to enjoy the mid-week classes offered at Bethel. Mother Genice, as we affectionately called her, was my favorite teacher. She knew how to take the Bible and make it relatable to issues I was dealing with. Mother Genice regularly welcomed the younger women from the church into her home. She would share the Bible and her life with us. Being a woman and growing up in the South meant that she had experienced her fair share of adversity. As a young woman, she had stared prejudice and discrimination right in the face, but she had refused to allow it to define her or to make her bitter. She had discovered something that was powerful enough to enable her to overcome the obstacles and challenges in her life. "I've come this far by faith," she would say. I'm not sure if she had even graduated from high school. By her own admission she wasn't "book smart." Her wisdom came from a source that was greater than herself. The teachings of Jesus were invaluable to her—they were quickly becoming an essential part of the transformation that was taking place in my life.

I could sit and listen to her stories and to her teaching the Bible for hours. The Bible had enough drama to rival *All My Children*, my favorite soap opera at the time. It was also full of practical advice. As a new Christian and a new wife, I had a lot to learn. I welcomed her guidance. However, on one particular evening, I wasn't prepared for the life lesson she broached.

Forgiveness.

She went on to explain all about divine reciprocity— *If you forgive the failures of others your heavenly father will also forgive you.* But the opposite was also true.

The more she talked, the more uneasy I became. My palms began to sweat and my stomach was in knots. No matter how much I fidgeted in the pew and tried to adjust my position, those words kept replaying in my mind.

I knew that these weren't her words. I tried even harder to ignore what I had just heard, but I couldn't. I knew exactly who it was that I needed to forgive, but I wasn't ready.

God didn't let up on me even though I was uncomfortable. Mother Genice began to sound like Charlie Brown's teacher—a meaningless hum. God's voice grew stronger, but not in a forceful way, just in a way that let me know this was something He wasn't going to let me ignore.

God, are we really doing this here and now? I don't want to deal with this. You know how painful my childhood had been and how deeply I've been hurt by my parents. I didn't want to allow myself to be vulnerable again.

Christa, God kept nudging. *You've allowed Me to do some difficult things in your heart already.*

It was true. A lot had changed in a short period of time. *But isn't that good enough, God?*

He was silent. He didn't have to answer me. It was going to take courage to do what I thought He was asking me to do.

"God, I can't even say the word out loud." I spoke into the air, hoping He could hear me as I struggled to say the word *forgive.* "Can't we stop with the spiritual surgery already? Can't we postpone this for a few more years?"

More silence. After what felt like forever, I spoke again.

"Okay, I guess You're not going to change Your mind on this one. It's clear You want me to *forgive.* There, I said it! But forgive my parents? How?" *This is not humanly possible. I don't even know where to begin,* I said under my breath as if God couldn't hear me.

I know it's not humanly possible, God pushed back. *You can't do this on your own, but I'll walk you through this. I have already given you the support you need—Mother Genice, Gloria, and Pastor Hunt have been placed in your life to help you. I'm always here too, Christa.*

"But they haven't even acknowledged their failures," I argued. "If I forgive them, I'll be letting them off the hook. Then they'll just hurt me again."

The voice sounded again. *You're going to have to trust Me and let Me deal with the rest.*

Still, I wasn't convinced that forgiveness was possible.

Christa, if you hold on to the unforgiveness and bitterness that you have against your parents, you will stay stuck in the pain. You won't be fully able to move forward into the future that I have planned for you. You've been praying to be free from your past. This is the next step toward that freedom. Forgiveness isn't easy, but I'm right here with you.

It was obvious that I needed to walk through this. After much agonizing, I relented, crying to God, "I want to be free from this—all of it. Take away this pain and resentment." I wanted to be a healthy wife and, someday, mother. I realized that I couldn't be emotionally healthy unless I was willing to work through my issues. How was I going to be able to let go of the anger and disappointment I had carried for so long?

Continue to trust Me and allow Me to guide you.

And with that, the process of forgiving my mother and father began.

22

OH NO, NOT AGAIN

Bethel was the place where my soul began to heal. I finally felt as if I belonged.

Gloria and I started spending a lot of time together outside of Sunday mornings. She and Pastor Hunt were the first married couple that I had an opportunity to get to know up close. They provided me examples of what a healthy family should look like. But Gloria was candid about the fact that they weren't perfect by any stretch of imagination—perfection didn't exist in real life. She was honest and open, sharing some of her own personal struggles with me.

"Bill and I almost got a divorce that first year we were married," she said, showing me the actual divorce papers.

I was taken aback. *You mean to say that even pastors have relational issues?* There had been a time in their marriage where she and Pastor Hunt had *irreconcilable differences—an irremediable breakdown of their marriage.* I didn't know exactly what all that meant, but I knew that it was bad enough to make them question their future together.

"I was so insecure," she explained. "I'd threaten to divorce him at least once a week. I guess he got tired of trying to convince me that the reason he had chosen me, over all the other sisters who wanted to marry him, was because he loved me."

Her admissions of imperfection made me feel less alone. She knew what it was like to struggle with feelings of insecurity and low self-esteem. "One day," she went on, "your pastor came home with these papers in his hand and gave me an ultimatum. 'If you tell me that you want a divorce one more time, I'm going to sign these papers.' After he did that," she said, "I never spoke of divorcing him again, although he's made me mad enough to consider murdering him."

We both laughed. She was a real person who had real challenges, just like everyone else.

Over time, the conversations between us went beyond just marital advice. We began having conversations about living our lives with purpose. Where I grew up, people were focused on getting by day-to-day. It was a struggle to put food on the table and keep the lights on. However, after having joined Bethel, I began to realize that there was more to life than just surviving. God intended for us to live meaningful lives. We were designed to make a significant impact.

Aside from their work in the ministry, Gloria was a registered nurse, and Pastor Hunt worked for a local utility company. They both had great jobs, so neither of them were being paid for their work at the church. Their motivations for serving the community weren't financial. They both felt a calling that had led them to the little church in Oak Park. The work was challenging, but their vision for the spiritual rebirth of the residents of Oak Park community superseded all the challenges.

Part of their vision for Oak Park was to develop programs for children and youth in the community. After some persuasion, I decided to join their efforts, despite my lack of experience with children.

I was entrusted with teaching the seven- and eight-year-old students in Sunday school. From the start, things didn't seem to be working out well.

Kids are smarter than we adults give them credit for. They recognized my inexperience right away—like sharks being drawn to blood. You can imagine why my assignment was short lived. After a month or so I was being reassigned. Thankfully, the Hunts realized I might be better suited to volunteer in some other capacity.

"We are sitting on a gold mine," Pastor Hunt said, encouraging his young congregants to invest in our neighborhood by purchasing property there. "One day people will flock back to Oak Park. Mark my words." He was predicting a phenomenon we now call gentrification.

In the spring of that year, we started a building-fund campaign, so that when the time was right, the church would be in a financial position to purchase a piece of nearby real estate too. Pastor Hunt had his eyes on a few of the properties that sat adjacent to the church. The building next door to us had sat empty for several years until, one day, a bail bonds company started leasing the space. Pastor Hunt was outraged.

"Having this sort of business located right next door to our church is sending the wrong message to the community—especially our youth. We have to do something about this."

He had every right to be incensed. He knew the residents of Oak Park deserved better.

Oak Park hadn't had a grocery store in the area for years— residents were forced to purchase necessities, like bread and milk, from the local liquor store, at double the price. One would also have to be brave enough to navigate through whatever criminal activities were taking place right in front of the liquor store. Residents were exhausted—there didn't seem to be much hope that things would ever improve.

Oak Park was plagued with similar issues as the neighborhoods that I had grown up in. We were forced to look outside of our community for anything good—food, education, medical attention— the options that were available to us in our own neighborhood were bleak. But Pastor Hunt believed that we could make a difference in Oak Park. Although he knew that eradicating the inequities that had existed there for years was going to require something radical.

To make matters worse, we were convinced that our new bail bonds neighbors were selling drugs next door, although we couldn't prove it. Pastor Hunt asked the congregation to begin praying that, by some miracle, we could raise the money needed to acquire the building. Our congregation was made up of mostly seniors who were on fixed incomes. There were a few younger families sprinkled in, but we were just starting our families, so we didn't have much in the way of resources either. Purchasing the property, with the intention of transforming it into an uplifting space for the community, seemed daunting. But Pastor Hunt believed that God could still work miracles. With just a little bit of faith, anything was possible.

One Sunday afternoon, the gentleman who ran the bail bonds company joined us for service. As the collection plate made its way around the church, the neighbor we believed to be involved in drug dealing discreetly slipped a wad of cash into the offering plate before departing.

Despite our suspicion that the generous donation may have come from illegal sources, we offered up praises for the unexpected windfall. In hindsight I must admit that our behavior was somewhat hypocritical. We were okay with using drug money, if it meant we could do some good with it. We continued praying that the man next door would either move or change his occupation—God had a better purpose for the building and for his life, we were sure of it.

We never saw our neighbor in church again, but soon thereafter the building became vacant. Pastor Hunt felt certain God was moving. He called a meeting with key leadership and some of our senior members, rallying us together to make the *faith purchase*. The surprise offering became seed money and a few months later we opened *The Academy*. The monies were used for good!

The Academy was a Pre-K program that mostly served single, working moms. Gloria was the school's director. She was passionate about creating a positive atmosphere for children in the community, realizing the importance of early childhood education and development. The Academy focused on the students' educational needs, as well as their emotional wellbeing.

It was important to Gloria that children in Oak Park had the same access to educational opportunities that other children living in more affluent areas had. No expense was spared to make sure that our students were prepared to thrive once they graduated from *The Academy*. It brought a ray of hope to the community.

Despite the progress we made, there was still a considerable amount of work to be done. Pastor Hunt believed in the grassroots efforts of going door to door—block by block. They spent many weekends canvassing the neighborhood, meeting people, praying with them, and inviting them to church.

Determined to get Guss and me involved, he asked us to join the outreach team. At the time, Guss was focusing all of his energy on basketball, but if Pastor Hunt ever decided to offer something in that arena, he promised to be all in.

After the whole Sunday School fiasco, I was eager to discover a place where my gifting could be best utilized. Pastor Hunt was certain that I would be a good fit for the weekend canvassing team. I agreed to accompany them on that following week. I was a little nervous about meeting folks in the neighborhood. I didn't know what to expect, but at least I felt more comfortable talking to adults than I did teaching kids.

The Saturday morning sessions started bright and early. We gathered for a quick word of prayer at the church and off we went. We walked several blocks, meeting people in the neighborhood, many of whom had lived there for years. They had seen the neighborhood decline. Residents spoke openly to us about the challenges of gang violence, joblessness, and all the other vices that plagued Oak Park.

I really enjoyed the community engagement. The day felt rewarding. Until, that is, we neared McClatchy Park.

My nervousness turned into full-on panic when I realized that McClatchy Park was a place where known gang members regularly gathered. It had only been a few short years since my cousin and I had almost lost our lives, simply because he had worn the wrong color clothing.

I looked down the street and all I saw was a sea of red. I panicked. I glanced down to see what I was wearing that day.

Whew. I was wearing black, which had no gang affiliation that I knew of.

I looked over to make sure the Hunts weren't breaking any code of ethics either. I breathed a sigh of relief. They were safe too. Praying for the neighbors was one thing, but I hadn't planned on us praying with gang members.

"Uh . . . are we heading back?" I nervously asked.

"Yeah, we are just about done," Pastor Hunt replied. "Once we talk to the crew at the park."

I shuddered. *The crew at the park was dangerous and scary.* I was surprised that Pastor Hunt hadn't known that.

How could he work in this neighborhood and not know that engaging with gang members was serious business? One misstep could cost our lives. I didn't think it was wise to mess with the group of guys at the park. We had done our good deeds for the day, and we should head back to the church before our good fortune ran out.

We were too close to turn and run—that might incite something altogether different. So, against my better judgment, we kept walking. I braced myself.

"Hello." Pastor Hunt approached the group of red-clad young people, with almost no regard for personal space and social etiquette.

I became even more nervous.

"I'm Pastor Hunt. I'm the new pastor of the brick church around the corner, on Broadway, near the bank. This is my wife, Gloria, and one of our church members. We are out walking the neighborhood, hoping to get to know some of the residents. We're inviting people to the church."

While he rattled off the service times, I waited for the young men to cuss Pastor Hunt out. Or worse.

"Yeah we know that church," one of them answered. "We just might do that."

It seemed like he was the leader, since he spoke for the entire group.

"Can we pray with you?" Gloria asked.

This time, I thought for sure that we had pushed too hard. We should have left when the leader agreed to consider coming to church. But before he could respond, Gloria began praying.

"Father, these are your sons. We ask that You would bless them. Please protect them and keep them safe. Oh, and one last thing—remind them that they are loved by You."

When she finished praying, Pastor Hunt and Gloria continued talking with the young men for a few more moments. I stood by quietly. Finally we headed back to the church.

I couldn't believe that people in the neighborhood had been so receptive and open, especially the group of men at the park.

I had misjudged them, lumping them all together. I hadn't seen them as people—but gang members.

Eventually, my desire to see transformation happen in lives of the residents of Oak Park grew beyond the Saturday morning prayer walks. I was beginning to understand that we were more alike than we were different. We all want to be seen, valued, and loved.

If God loved *me* enough to pursue me and to transform my life, then no one was out of the parameters of His reach. Pastor Hunt and Gloria were right. Every one of us has been made for something great.

Over time, I was becoming less intimidated by the people in the neighborhood. I was beginning to feel like my purpose somehow involved sharing the message that no matter who you are and where you've been, the arms of God are outstretched toward you.

One Saturday afternoon, one of the "ladies of the streets" walked into the church. I had been praying for this particular group of women. My heart broke for them—for her. The fact that she was now standing at our doorstep was, in my opinion, nothing short of a miracle. God was listening to my prayers.

More importantly, it was a sign that He loved this woman. He hadn't turned a deaf ear to her cries, nor to her pain. Her life mattered to Him.

I quickly introduced myself. I couldn't help but wonder what sort of trauma she had endured. What had her childhood been like? What had led her to such a low point that she was willing to sell away her dignity for a few dollars?

"My name is Charity," she said, stammering over her words. Her name embodied the essence of all that I had come to know about God. *Charitas—signifying the highest form of love. The disposition of generosity and benevolent goodwill, extended to us from God.* The tragic irony of it all was that Charity seemed to have no idea how God felt about her.

I tried to convince her to sit for a moment, but she refused.

"I can't stay," she said. "I have to go back to work."

I had spent the past year watching Pastor Hunt and Gloria caring for people in the community. They weren't afraid because they knew that helping hurting people was what God had called them to do.

I grabbed Charity's hands and squeezed them tightly, as if I could somehow transfer God's love to her through my own hands. I offered up a prayer for protection and provision and told her that I hoped our paths would soon cross again. With that, she turned and left.

23

GOING PRO

After Guss finished playing basketball at Sacramento State, he decided to see if he had what it took to play professionally. As a young boy, he imagined himself playing in the NBA alongside basketball greats like Julius Erving. "Pistol" Pete Maravich and Gus Williams were among his all-time favorite players. He idolized Gus Williams so much that when he was in high school he insisted that his friends and family start calling him Guss instead of Albert. No one protested and the name stuck from then on.

The CBA (Continental Basketball Association), a minor league for men, was hosting an open tryout in Los Angeles, of all places. I was excited to go home, even if it was just for a few days. I immediately called Valorie to share the good news that Guss might be "going Pro." She was excited, and we made plans to catch up while I was in LA.

"You and Guss can crash at our house," she said, but Guss had decided that we would stay at a motel near the venue. LA traffic was always a nightmare, and he didn't want anything to ruin his chances of making the team.

"I want to be among the first players to show up, so that I can make a good impression on the coaches."

Of course, I was willing to sacrifice spending a little extra time with Valorie. Anything to give him an advantage.

I was also looking forward to seeing the family. I hadn't been to LA since Valorie and Tyrone's wedding. We had been plenty busy settling into being newlyweds and adjusting to the new rhythms of marriage. My volunteer commitments at the church continued to expand, which, along with work, kept me busy.

Guss completed the application and mailed in the required hundred-dollar entry fee. Finances were still tight, but if this put him one step closer to his dreams then it would all be worth it.

A few weeks later, we drove to LA for what we hoped would be an opportunity of a lifetime. Secretly, I tried to bargain with God.

"If you let Guss make the team, I promise we will give more money to the building campaign, and I'll even teach Sunday School again, although you know that's not my gifting. I think I could even persuade Guss to join us on our Saturday morning community walks."

I'm not sure what else I promised on that day but I threw it all out there, hoping God would take the bait. Funny thing is, He already knows what we are going to do before we do it. He knew I couldn't keep all those promises I had made. Besides, His plans for our lives had already been determined. I didn't need to barter with him.

I decided to tag along with Guss to the gym, for moral support and to check out his competition. At the registration table, we were met by a woman with a less than pleasant attitude.

"Name?" She said matter-of-factly, without even looking up at us.

"Guss Armstead."

"Here you go. You're number two twenty-five. The gym's that way."

I turned to follow him.

"Excuse me," she said to me, pointing to an overhead sign that read *Players Only* in big bold letters. "You can't go in there with him. No visitors allowed. That means no moms, aunties, or girlfriends."

Or wives? I thought to myself. I didn't argue so as not to make a scene. I kissed Guss goodbye, wished him luck, and told him to call me when he was done.

I spent that afternoon at Mama Shirley's, hanging out with Tyrone, Valorie, and a host of her cousins. We played Spades and Dominoes, while Mama Shirley did what she always did best—whipping up something delectable for us to munch on. Their family gatherings were never short on great food and great company. That afternoon, we were our usual trash talking selves. I was always paired up against Valorie and Tyrone with one of her cousins. I'm not sure how our friendship had outlasted our cutthroat games of Spades and Dominoes.

No matter how much fun we were having, I couldn't get my mind off of Guss. I began to imagine my future as a pro-baller's wife. More money would certainly be nice. Maybe we could afford to buy new furniture or possibly purchase a home. I definitely wanted to get rid of our Goodwill couch. Being able to raise a family in a neighborhood that offered good schools, and that was safe, didn't seem like too much to wish for. I didn't want my children to have to live in fear or to witness the things I had witnessed while growing up.

While I wanted Guss to follow his dreams, I was anxious about the impact his new career might have on our lives. The thought of having to move to another city made me a little anxious. I enjoyed living in Sacramento—while it had its pockets of problems, there were still neighborhoods that felt safe enough to rear children in, in the future. I wasn't sure how I felt about the possibility of having to uproot our lives and I dreaded the idea of leaving our new church family behind. The people at Bethel had become our community. I had found a sense of purpose there—we both had. I wasn't sure if we could find a church like Bethel. I wondered if we'd even fit in at a new church, in a new city.

Guss called to say that he was ready to be picked up. The tension in the car was palpable on our ride back to the motel. I couldn't read the situation. Maybe he had done so well at the tryout that he was worried about our impending move too?

"How'd it go?" I asked.

"There were more than a hundred other players at my position who tried out today. The coaches will let us know whether we made the cut tomorrow."

I had no idea how many spots were available but I hoped for the best.

The following morning, he received the disappointing news that out of the hundreds of players who were there that weekend, only two would be invited back for a second tryout. Unfortunately, he did not make the cut.

He had always been aware that becoming a professional basketball player was a formidable challenge. Some players were willing to devote years to the process. But Guss had always maintained that he wouldn't be one of those players. He promised he'd know when it was time to call it quits. He was definitely at that crossroads now. Should he keep pursuing his hoop dreams? Or was it time to come to terms with the inevitable? *Retirement.*

A few weeks later, we sat down to discuss the tryout and the implications it had on our future. True to his word, Guss had made his peace with the fact that his basketball playing days were over. It was time for new dreams.

Eventually, Pastor Hunt did persuade him to join a church basketball league. Their games were a comedy of errors. Most of the guys on Bethel's team were out of their element and had never really played basketball before, except maybe in their driveways.

But thankfully, as one door was closing in his life, another door seemed to be opening. Soon, Guss became a graduate assistant coach for the Sac State basketball team. Over the course of time, he also began training and consulting players on the side.

Guss and a good friend named Dennis had an amazing opportunity suddenly drop into their laps. They were asked to take over the management of the Sacramento Pro-Am, an NBA sponsored league that featured current NBA players as well as some of the most recognizable basketball names in Sacramento's history, most of whom had been high school legends in the area. The Pro-Am afforded players who were coming out of college an opportunity to hone their skills by playing against current NBA talents. Players like LaSalle Thompson—the six foot ten, 250-pound superstar center for the Sacramento Kings—were involved in the league. Tank, as his friends called him, was a gentle giant off the court, but on the court, he was a defensive nightmare.

That previous summer, Tank and Guss had been on the same team and had hit it off right away, sharing similar passions—basketball and good food. Being the fifth overall pick of the 1982 NBA draft had its rewards. Tank was a highly touted and celebrated basketball player, but quite often people solely perceived him as an athlete and failed to recognize his other qualities beyond the court. He was a kind-hearted and compassionate person who was willing to give away the shirt off his back to someone in need. To most folks, he was a celebrity, but to us he was a friend.

Guss wasn't playing basketball anymore, but his relationship with Tank and the other Sacramento Kings players allowed him into the spaces he had dreamed of being.

Guss and Dennis made the decision to establish a formal partnership and a few months later, Pros N Motion was born. One of their very first big projects was a collaboration with a company called Gus Macker. Gus Macker was the fictitious name of a guy named Scott McNeal. His company was the first of its kind to host three-on-three basketball tournaments nationwide. Guss and Dennis signed on to help organize Sacramento's first city-wide outdoor three-on-three tournament, which became a huge success.

It was a great start, but we both knew that he couldn't hang his hat on one successful weekend. He would need to invest a lot more time and energy into building up his company.

Guss kept his day job as the manager of a sports memorabilia store called Fan Fever. Fan Fever became a haven for NBA stars and die-hard enthusiasts alike. Tank, Ed Pinckney, Harold Pressley, Derek Smith, and Kenny Smith (who were not related) regularly hung out with Guss at Fan Fever. Fans would line up in front of the store for hours to get their hands on the newest and most popular Starter jacket or their favorite team gear. The walls at Fan Fever were adorned with personally autographed photos of NBA players, reminiscent of what you might find at a popular foodie spot. The crew at Fan Fever were as beloved as the iconic cast of the '80s sitcom *Cheers*. "It was a place where everybody knew your name. And they're always glad you came."

On a regular basis, you could catch Tank and some of the other players hanging out at the store, talking trash with Guss about last night's game. The owner of the store, Big Earl, stood six foot six inches tall and looked like he was a retired basketball player or coach himself. He loved the fact that Guss had relationships with the players. It was great for business for him.

The location Guss managed was the most popular and the most lucrative of the chain of stores. That year, Guss was named "Manager of the Year." But in the back of his mind, he had his sights set on something greater—being an entrepreneur. He had always envisioned working for himself and had never been much for taking directions from other people. It was the reason he hadn't followed in his father's footsteps and joined the military.

Guss's new ventures gave me opportunities to do what I loved— meeting new people. I became friends with several of the players' wives and girlfriends, and we were soon sharing stories about our lives and bonding over fashion and family. When it was appropriate, I'd tell them about how I had come to faith.

We started attending NBA games pretty regularly. Sometimes Guss and I would show up to the will-call at the arena to pick up our tickets and discover that several of the guys on the team had left tickets for us. One night we counted—sixteen tickets had been left for just the two of us. That had to be a record of some sort. It felt like the people at the Arena were always sizing us up and trying to figure out who we were.

"Yaw must be important—somebody really wants you at this game. Mr. Pressley, Mr. Smith, and Mr. Thompson have all left tickets for you."

Guss and I enjoyed front-row seats to the lives we only dreamed of. However, "success" looked different up close. Fame and riches come with their own set of obstacles to overcome. Success didn't necessarily guarantee happiness, as most people, including Guss and I, had imagined it would.

After the games, we'd wait in the players' family lounge while the guys showered and finished up with their media interviews. This gave us the opportunity to see other NBA stars up close. They had to pass right by the family lounge area to get to the team bus.

One evening while we were waiting on Tank to finish showering, I caught a glimpse of Michael Jordan out of the corner of my eye. This was *big*. I mean *huge*. He was walking right up to us, as if we had already met before. I was ecstatic. I had mentioned to Tank that I wanted to meet him someday, but I didn't think he had taken me seriously. It's not everyday that you get to meet a legend like him. He was arguably the GOAT. You know, "greatest of all time."

The moment felt surreal. I began rehearsing what I might say as he introduced himself to us. I didn't want to stumble over my words. The last thing I wanted to do was to come across as a backstage groupie. If you were granted access to the back of the arena, it was taboo to ask for an autograph, but it was permissible to greet your favorite players.

Just as I was about to open my mouth to say hello, I realized that Michael Jordan wasn't coming to meet me after all. He was trying to exit the arena so that he could board the bus.

He did, however, give me a head nod. He was as tall and as charismatic in person as he was in his Nike commercials, co-starring the famous movie director Spike Lee. Even though I didn't get his autograph, I'll never forget the night that I *almost* met Michael Jordan. Talk about six degrees of separation.

Tank began inviting Guss and me over to his home for dinner and the holidays. We enjoyed spending Thanksgiving with him and his family, and enjoyed the delicious meal prepared by his mom, who was an amazing cook. I could only imagine the large quantities of food Tank had consumed as a teen.

Guss continued coaching and training players. He discovered that he had a gift when it came to identifying talent and for helping them to further develop their skills. He was fully immersed in the business of basketball.

Coaching players wasn't really work for him at all. It was more like living out his best dream. Financially, things were improving, but more importantly we were feeling good about the direction our lives were heading.

24

FAILURE
TO APPEAR

I had always enjoyed helping people, so I got a job working retail at Macy's department store in downtown Sacramento. On the weekends I continued volunteering at Bethel. I still loved singing in the choir and serving on special projects involving the community.

I continued to pray for more opportunities to reach the *ladies of the streets*. I thought about Charity and I prayed for her often, even though I hadn't seen her since that day she stumbled into the church. I wasn't even sure I'd recognize her if I saw her walking down the street, but one thing was for sure, I would never forget her name.

Over time I met several other women like Charity. Eager to share my story with them, I tried to find creative ways to connect. Sometimes that would mean following them down the street as they worked. I'd be talking to them while they were literally being flagged down by customers. It sounds crazy, and I'm sure the ladies questioned my stability. Who would dare have the audacity to chase down sex workers while they were on the job? I wasn't normally this bold—I just wanted these women to encounter the same love that I had experienced. The love of the Father couldn't be compared to any other love I had ever known. I wanted them to know that they were loved beyond measure—unconditionally. After all, had it not been for my neighbors, James and Gladys, who had gone out of their way to meet two college kids and to invite us to church, Guss and I might not have ended up at Bethel. Who knows where we'd be?

One day, while leaving church, I was pulled over by a police officer. He wrote me a ticket for not wearing my seatbelt. The fine was pretty hefty. Since Guss and I didn't have much in the way of extra cash, I opted to do community service in lieu of paying a fine. My assignment was to pick up the trash on the side of the road with all the other traffic offenders—orange vest and all.

Somehow, I ended up missing my first court-appointed assignment. I called to reschedule right away. Only this time the clerk on the phone informed me that I would need to come to court to appeal to a judge for an extension.

I vividly remember that my court date fell on a Friday, because it conflicted with my work schedule. I was so new to the job that I was still on probation. I was forced to call my supervisor at work, to explain the whole embarrassing traffic ticket fiasco to her. I didn't want her to think that I was playing hooky in order to have an extended weekend off.

The courtroom was full. There must have been at least fifty cases ahead of mine. The stories people concocted to get out of paying fines kept me entertained. Many folks had only committed minor offenses, like riding on the bus without paying the fare or breaking newly enacted seatbelt laws, like I had done. Some of the offenses were more serious in nature. The gentlemen's case that was heard before mine involved a DUI.

The judge seemed to be in a fairly good mood that day. He had granted leniency in the case of the drunk driver. I was hoping for that same grace.

But my original ticket had turned into a *Failure to Appear.* I now owed the courts an exorbitant amount of money. I thought the best approach was to keep things simple and to be honest. Finally, I was called to approach the bench.

"In the case of driving without a seatbelt how do you plead, Mrs. Armstead?" the judge asked.

"Guilty, your honor."

"And in the case of the Failure to Appear, how do you plead?"

"Guilty, your honor."

I did have a reasonable explanation for that infraction. I had made a minor scheduling error, which we could quickly remedy. All I needed to do was to set a new date for Community Service, so that I could get back to work.

His gavel come crashing down. The events that transpired next were a blur. I thought I heard him explain that I was to step into the next room to pay the additional fine. As I began walking in that direction, the court bailiff approached me and asked me to put my hands behind my back. Then he handcuffed me.

I was in such shock that I resisted for a second.

"What's going on? Why are you handcuffing me? I'm only here to get reassigned to Community Service," I pleaded.

"Ma'am, you are under arrest. The judge has remanded you to ten days in the county jail."

And with that, I was removed from the courtroom and placed in a jail cell. Like a full fledged criminal.

I couldn't believe what was happening to me. I was being arrested for a traffic ticket and would have to spend ten days in jail for not wearing my seatbelt? I couldn't wrap my mind around the fact that I was going to jail. I might have deserved to spend ten days in jail for selling weed in the girls' bathroom back in junior high, but this was egregious.

I was sure to lose my job for this. And how was I going to explain this to Guss?

The moment was surreal.

Pointing to the pay phone in the cell, the bailiff said, "You get one phone call. Use it wisely."

I called Guss, but he didn't pick up. By that time, I was shaking uncontrollably and bawling my eyes out. I was afraid that I wasn't even going to have the opportunity to let my husband know that I was in jail.

With cracking voice, I called out to the officer on duty and explained that my husband hadn't picked up the phone. She gave me permission to make another call. This time I called Gloria. I was crying so hard that she couldn't understand what I was saying.

"You're where? Doing what?"

"I'm in jail. I got arrested for missing my Community Service appointment and the judge sentenced me to ten days in jail," I said, still sobbing. "I tried calling Guss but he didn't answer . . . I only get one call and I didn't know who else to reach out to, so I called you . . . would you at least pray for me . . .? I'm so scared . . . and could you keep calling Guss? He's at work, and he needs to know what's happened to me."

I spoke in one big rapid-fire sentence, hoping I could tell her everything she needed to know, before we were cut off because the calls were timed.

She was silent for a moment, then she prayed with a fervency, asking God for my protection. When she finished praying, she told me that God had given her a vision of me in what seemed to be dark cave. "The place is dark and you're going to be afraid, but while I was praying, God showed me that He's going to protect you. You're not going to be there the entire time. You're going to get out of the dark cave in three days. I'm not sure why this has happened, but you're going to be all right. God is going to keep you safe."

It was hard to end the call. She told me that she would continue praying for me over the next few days.

I was made to do all the typical things a person who's been arrested has to do. They took all my personal belongings. In exchange, I was given a sterile gray outfit and some under garments that appeared to have already been worn and rewashed.

After a long wait, I was eventually escorted upstairs to an official jail cell. It was a small space with two beds, a sink, and a toilet. Nothing else.

For the first few hours I was alone in my cell, but later that evening I got a cellmate. When you are confined to a six-by-eight-foot cell with someone, it's hard to ignore them. The young woman and I made small talk and asked typical questions of one another. The most important one was, of course, how we had ended up in jail in the first place. Her offense seemed minor as well, although she did admit to having been arrested on one other occasion. She gave me her version of the "dos and don'ts" of jail and of what to expect over the next ten days. I was grateful for her advice, but I explained that I would be going home on Sunday, *just as Gloria said.*

She humored me. "Well, at least you'll only need your husband to put a little bit of money on your books."

When I first arrived, one of the intake guards explained that I would need money on my books to buy extra personal items like special snacks, hygiene items, and cigarettes. Thankfully, I didn't smoke.

I finally dozed off. We were awakened by a loud bell and my name being called over the PA system. "Christa Armstead, roll out," the voice said.

Since I wasn't as familiar with prison lingo, I turned to my cellmate for interpretation.

"It means you're leaving," she explained.

I was elated! I was going home! Surprisingly, I was being released from jail even earlier than Gloria had predicted. But that excitement quickly turned into disappointment. I wasn't going home early, instead I was being transferred to another facility. The Rio Consumnes Correctional Center (RCCC) was located in the neighboring community of Elk Grove. I was handed a pamphlet that described the facility. "The goal of RCCC was to prevent escapes and wrongful releases and to increase the vocational and educational opportunities for inmates confined in their facilities."

There it was written in black in white. The goal of RCCC was to prevent me from being wrongfully released and to somehow rehabilitate me in a matter of three days. Why hadn't the goal been to keep individuals like me from having to come to a place like this in the first place? In my opinion there was nothing rehabilitating or humane about a system that threw people in jail for seatbelt tickets.

About fifty of us boarded a bus for the minimum-security facility. Some of the women seemed to know one another already. One of the women on the bus was engaged in a friendly conversation with the officers who were escorting us to our new accommodations. They joked with her about being back again, as if she were a frequent hotel guest. She seemed to be pretty chummy with the officers, and I figured she might make a good ally. I certainly might need one where I was going. I sat back, quietly trying to absorb it all.

When we arrived at RCCC, we had to be strip searched again, only this time it wouldn't be in a private space. We were made to remove our clothing in front of the officers and all the other women who were on the bus that day. It was the single most dehumanizing experience of my entire life.

After we had finished redressing ourselves, we were handed a few toiletries, a stack of linens, and a few more items of clothing. Then we were escorted to our living quarters. I was placed in a huge room that held about seventy or so women. The space was dingy and filled with an overwhelming scent of pine cleaner that had been used excessively. It wasn't a small cell, like the one I had been in earlier at the County Jail. It had wall to wall bunk beds that reminded me of a summer camp dormitory. Only I'm sure we weren't going to roast marshmallows around a campfire or sing B-I-N-G-O was his name-o. A late model television was mounted in the corner of the room and some of the ladies already seemed to be arguing about what they wanted to watch. We at least had more than one bathroom stall that was thankfully private. I went and found an empty bunk to claim as mine and immediately started trying to build some alliances, even though I believed that I was going home soon.

I learned a few of the other girls' stories and explained how I had ended up in jail for a seatbelt ticket.

"What? That's messed up," one girl said. "I don't think I've heard of that before."

I was just as dumbfounded as she was, but several of the women seemed to be there for committing petty offenses like me. We were experiencing the injustices of a broken system.

That afternoon I participated in a Bible study that was offered every Saturday. I had been invited by another bunk mate. She shared that she wasn't very religious but she attended the group to pass the time. I didn't tell her that I had a different reason for joining the study. *My safety.*

The woman leading the study opened with a few hymns before she spoke. We all joined her as if we were one big choir. I probably sang a little louder than I should have, but music always gave me comfort and I was certainly in need of it that weekend.

My singing drew the attention of a few of the women. When we got back to the barracks, we struck up conversations about music. That eventually led to a conversation about God and about Bethel. For some reason, I felt safe enough to share that I was involved in the choir at my church. I noticed that one of the women raised an eyebrow when I mentioned the name of the church and where it was located, but I kept talking. I was doing everything I could to try to make the best out of an unbelievably difficult situation. *Maybe one of the women might eventually come visit Bethel?* It was a long shot, but at least they would know where we were located and that they had an open invitation to join us there. I'd also make sure to add them to the prayer list when I went home, which I hoped would be soon.

Later that evening, one of the women asked if she could speak with me privately, away from the group. She began telling me that she lived near the church and would often pass by it. She shared some deeper things about her family and her long battle with drug addiction, which resulted in her losing her children to the system. Listening to her story broke my heart. She had experienced years of trauma and, I'm sure, abuse. Although she didn't go into that part of her story, the telling signs were there.

At the close of our conversation, I asked for her permission to pray with her. She agreed. It dawned on me that we had been talking all this time but that I hadn't asked her name. I always wanted to learn a person's name before praying with them. It was important for me to speak their name out loud to God so that they would know He was listening—and that He knew them by name.

"My name is Charity," she shared.

I was speechless! Wait! Is this really *Charity?* The same Charity that I had been praying for over the past few months? I hadn't recognized her without her makeup and the long blonde wig she wore when she was working the streets.

In that moment I saw her—the real her. Not what she did for a living—but the woman she was underneath the layers of life.

I'm certain that I rambled for the next ten minutes—trying to explain to her that she and I had meet before. She didn't recall having attended a service at Bethel, but she did recall passing the church on many occasions while working. I tried putting into words how much God loved her and that she might possibly be the reason that a seatbelt ticket had landed me in jail.

I wasn't sure whether it had been divine intervention or a broken justice system that allowed our paths to cross again—in jail of all places. And I was certain that one conversation couldn't erase all the years of neglect and the pain she had endured. But I was unequivocally convinced that God loved Charity.

When we finished praying, I wrote my number on a small piece of a paper I had torn from my Bible study notes and handed it to her.

"Come see us once you get out. I want you to meet everybody at the church," I said, hoping she'd take me up on it.

That next morning, I heard my name being called over the loudspeaker again. This time I really was going home. A few of the women who had befriended me on that weekend came up to say their goodbyes.

"Girl, your friend was right. You really are going home early. Can you put my name on the prayer list?" one of them said.

To be honest, their names faded as soon as I left that day. But there was one name I would never forget—*Charity.*

When I got home, I learned the full story of how I had gotten my sentence reduced by seven days. It was a miracle. Guss' attorney friend was somehow able to get in touch with a judge over the weekend. He explained my case, advocating for me to the courts.

"This woman hasn't ever committed a crime before. *At least not one that I had been caught doing.* She's a law-abiding citizen who serves her community. Her pastors and the people at her church can attest to her character."

The judge agreed to my early release on one condition. I had to report to the courts and pay a *one-thousand-dollar* fine, which our good friend Tank had generously given Guss. Not loaned—given. In all the years of our friendship, Tank never mentioned the money or my time in jail again.

25

BOYS IN THE HOOD

I n 1988, I gave birth to a baby boy. We named him Aaron Kelly Armstead. Guss didn't want a junior so we opted to give him his dad's middle name instead. My mother was like most grandmothers, possessing grandiose ideas as to what her first grandchild could aspire to. Before he'd uttered his first words, she'd already started calling him Mr. President! And she was dead serious. I think she actually believed that Aaron could be the first African American President of the United States.

While I thought the presidency was a stretch, I did pray that whatever path he chose in life would involve helping others.

Armond Kory, our second son, was born in August of 1990. Mondo, as we affectionately called him, came out of the womb with a fierce strength, with muscles already formed as a baby. He would speed around the house in his walker for hours, nearly running us over and never tiring.

Determined to rear our children in a safer place than The Jungle, Guss and I decided to permanently plant our roots in Sacramento where we did our best to support our growing family. We'd even managed to convince Valorie and Tyrone to finally leave LA and relocate near us, where the rent was cheaper and the world was kind.

Everything was coming together perfectly, especially now that I had my best friend at my side once again. Before long, she and Tyrone joined the church, attending Bethel's services along with us. Together, as young mothers, Valorie and I continued supporting one another through all the new challenges of our lives. We'd both left the past far behind.

Until one morning, while I was sleep-deprived and longing for rest, the phone blared, startling me out of my slumber. I snatched up the receiver so that, God forbid, its constant ringing wouldn't wake my little tribe.

"Hello," I said, quietly.

When the man on the phone addressed me by my maiden name, my heart skipped a beat. No one had addressed me that way in a few years.

"It's Christa Armstead now, sir."

"Well, Mrs. Armstead, our offices have been trying to get in touch with you," said the voice on the line.

"What offices?"

"Ma'am, I'm calling from the Los Angeles County District Attorney's Office. Were you the victim of a shooting back in 1984?"

Amidst the diapers and dishes of my current life, I'd forgotten all about that fateful evening when my cousin Gary and I came so close to death that we could almost touch it. I was so far removed from my past life in The Jungle that I'd completely blocked that incident out of my mind.

Guss and I weren't well-off by any stretch of the imagination, but one of the reasons we'd decided to settle in Sacramento was so none of our children, especially our sons, would have to end up like Ricky from the movie *Boyz n the Hood*.

I'd cried so hard when Ricky's character, played by Morris Chestnut, was gunned down by a gang member. Ricky was a football star who had earned a full ride scholarship to USC. The saddest part of the story was that Ricky wasn't even involved in gangs—he was an innocent victim. Thankfully, I was quickly consoled when the credits rolled, and I walked out of the theater knowing I'd see him again in his next film.

Sadly, that hadn't been the case with many of the young men I'd grown up with in LA. Death by violence was a common and harsh reality. I'll never forget the day that I learned that my childhood friend Lamar had been gunned down while walking home from the liquor store. This was the same store we'd frequented as kids. I wasn't supposed to hang out with boys back then. My aunts would have grounded me for weeks had they known. But despite their warnings, I'd often sneak out to ride skateboards with Lamar and Kenny, who happened to be together the day Lamar was murdered.

Lamar's mother nearly lost her mind after that. He was only sixteen years old at the time of his death. Life had been snatched away from her precious baby boy while he was still in his prime. Who knows what he could have achieved, had he not grown up in the wrong neighborhood? Perhaps he might have become a teacher, or a writer, or a great father? If only he had been given the opportunity to do so. We will never know.

Another friend, CP, had been stabbed to death by another teen while on his way home from school. The losses were too many to count.

"Christa, we are subpoenaing you to testify in a capital murder case."

I froze. They wanted me to come and testify against one of the suspects who had nearly killed my cousin Gary and me. The gang member who had shot up the Good Samaritan's house. This time his nefarious behavior had led to murder.

"We need your help in putting this guy away before he kills someone else. Would you be willing to come to LA and tell your story to a Grand Jury? We need you to help us get this menace off the streets."

"I don't think I can help you, sir. In my original statement to the police, I told the officer that I'd been standing by the window that night, but when the shooting began, we all hit the floor. I never saw the gunman's face, nor had I seen the car they drove away in. I wouldn't be much help." I said this as convincingly as possible, determined to avoid bringing this kind of danger into my new life with Guss, especially now that we had two children to protect.

But the man wasn't easily persuaded. "Couldn't you at least come and share about what that night did to you and your cousin? Says here you were all huddled up in a back bedroom, expecting to be killed at any moment when LAPD rescued you."

He was right about one thing. We'd all thought for sure they were going to kick the door in and finish the job. They seemed intent on killing Gary that night. Sure, the physical scars eventually went away, but the emotional ones never did. I could only imagine the impact that fateful night had on the woman and her children. She had endangered her entire family while trying to help complete strangers.

"Sir, I really would like to help you, but I have young children to take care of here in Sacramento."

"Then you owe it to them to put an end to this kind of violence." He said this as if my testimony could somehow change the systems and structures that were equally responsible for holding certain communities in its grip for years. Communities in which the social disparities and inequities had outweighed possibilities and opportunities for far too long. It was no secret that members of these communities eventually became casualties of injustices. As victims of extreme poverty, redlining, police brutality, and poor and failing school systems, they were usually left depleted of hope. It would take more than one testimony to put an end to this kind of violence.

"I'll talk it over with my husband," I said, with a sigh. "I'll get back to you."

Later that day when Guss got home, I told him about the strange call I'd received from the DA's offices. He quickly busted my "do-gooder's" bubble.

"The mother of my children ain't getting involved in no murder case," he said, matter-of-factly, quickly laying to rest any ideas I might have had about testifying against such a dangerous man. "You can tell him, or I can call him and tell him for you."

And that was that. Life went back to normal, and I focused on being a mother and a wife, leaving my past behind me.

A few years later, in March of 1992, our only daughter, Alexis Kamille, came into the world weighing almost nine pounds, as if she'd known she'd have to hold her own against a world of strong brothers.

"Babe, she has red hair just like you," Guss interjected, as delivery room nurses placed her on me so that I could nurse her for the first time and we could bond. "Now I have two favorite redheads in my life," Guss said, as he cooed and doted over his baby girl like nobody's business, even singing to her. *You are my sunshine, my only sunshine, you make me happy when skies are gray. You'll never know how much Dad loves you...*

I didn't mind sharing his affections with her. I was just grateful she had such a loving father, and I knew he would never leave us the way my father had done to my mother and me.

Soon after, Arik Kristian, the baby of the brood, burst onto the scene in 1993, at a whopping ten pounds, eleven ounces! We were certain that whatever he'd do in life, it would be *big!* At three months, he was already wearing clothes sized for a twelve-month-old.

Oh, how Alexis loved her little brother! "I help wit da baby, Mama," she'd say, as she'd try to fasten his diaper or help me feed *her* baby.

I've since run the numbers and estimated that I'd changed more than 40,000 diapers, prepared at least 6,000 meals, and read about 10,000 bedtime stories in those five years. Guss and I were wide-eyed, naive young parents who had underestimated the responsibilities of raising so many children. I wish someone had written a manual that could have prepared me for what I considered to be the most important assignment of my life—motherhood!

The commercials made things look so easy. Babies on TV always slept quietly, and they certainly didn't spit up or have diaper blowups. One of those diaper mishaps happened with Aaron, who peed all over my face and even gave himself a shower during one those earliest diapering sessions.

My mothering skills improved in time but raising four kids under the age of five was never easy. Life revolved around our children, as I believed it should. But this meant that keeping up with the things I loved to do became difficult. I had less time to volunteer with the community projects. Still, I tried to keep singing in the church choir, determined not to lose that connection to God. No matter how busy life became, I remained committed to using my gifts to serve Him.

"All choir members to the choir stand please for an A & B selection," our director would say.

That meant we'd be singing two songs. That might have been a treat for me at another phase of my life, but with so many babies needing to eat, it could prove a challenge. Especially when Brother Darris would get extra happy and carry those two songs on for what felt like hours.

One day, we'd repeated the chorus over and over again, and just as we got to the part of the hymn he liked to linger on, the front of my dress was suddenly soaking wet!

Oh no, I thought to myself, *it's time to nurse Arik.*

My nursing pads had failed me, and I was lucky I wasn't leading a solo that day! All eyes would have been on me, but for the wrong reasons.

Our lives were busy. Guss continued coaching and training basketball players. While he focused on earning income for the family, I dove into my life of being a wife and mother. I was determined that we would break dysfunctional, generational cycles and vowed never to repeat the past. I wanted my children to be reared by both their parents, as I had witnessed firsthand the countless difficulties of flying solo.

I had great admiration for the women in my family who'd raised their children alone. I realized that it took the exceptional strength and courage to be both a mother and father.

Parenting was not a job I ever wanted to do by myself. My father's absence had left a void so deep that it would take years to fill. I was thankful that Guss was there to provide stability for our family and to protect us. I never wanted any of my children to go through life feeling that kind of rejection and pain.

Over the next few years, Guss and I would have three focuses— family, faith, and sports (which unfortunately doesn't start with the letter *F*). When he first went into business for himself, things were hard. Back then, basketball training wasn't popular like it is today. When you have four children, someone always seems to need something. A pair of shoes, pants that aren't several inches too short, and of course, food—and plenty of it!

In those days, I'd go to the grocery store with twenty dollars in my pocket, hoping to feed our family of six for the week. Guss was still building his business. It was feast or famine for our family. When finances were really tight, I'd visit the local food pantry for help. I learned to get really creative with cans of pork and beans and Vienna sausages.

We didn't tell many people about the severity of our financial difficulties, but then again, we didn't have to. When my in-laws would come to visit, they'd bring bags of groceries with them. Once a woman from church asked to borrow our car keys, which I thought was a little strange. After church, we discovered that she had filled our little Hyundai with food that lasted for several weeks. God always provided for us. Although I admit I was embarrassed that the provisions came to us through the generosity of others.

A friend once told me that sort of attitude was prideful. I already had a lot of stuff that needed correcting. Geez, one more thing to add to my list of hang-ups?

"Just say thank you," she said. "You'll be able to do the same for someone else someday."

She had been where I was and had come out on the other side. The beauty of hindsight! God was teaching us. We were learning how to lean on Him and to trust Him with little. Guss and I were also learning how to focus on and to appreciate the things He had blessed us with—health, our family, a community, our faith, and so many more blessings that time or space wouldn't permit me to share.

Instead of being resentful about our difficulties, I tried learning from them instead. Maya Angelou, one of my favorite orators, once said, "No matter what happens or how bad it seems today, life does go on and it will be better tomorrow."

26

WELCOME BACK

The birth of our children had been a blessing to my relationship with Mama. We still had a lot of work to do, but in many ways her grandchildren became a catalyst for healing.

"Christa, I know I can't make up for all the damage I've done," Mama said, holding her youngest grandson in her arms. "I'm going to try to be a better grandmother than I was a mother. I promise."

Since becoming a mother, I was able to feel a greater empathy for Mama. Parenting was hard enough for people who hadn't been through all the hurtful traumas she'd endured. I couldn't imagine how difficult life had been for her.

I don't believe any parent sets out to intentionally hurt or damage their children, but personal demons can be hard to defeat. For many years, I had judged her for her shortcomings, but motherhood changed me. I now saw things from a different vantage point. It's hard to have empathy for someone until you have walked in their shoes. Frankly I was scared and that fear drove me to my knees!

The kids loved my mother. On summer breaks, we'd travel to LA. Mama would take the entire crew to amusement parks, zoos, and beaches. She took pride in the fact that she was healthy enough to keep up with them, and she loved to make their field trips educational. The USC Science Center was a *two for one* because it was located on a college campus. The kids could discover their inner awe and wonder, and Mama could basically conduct her own version of a college tour. It was never too early to start planting seeds about college in the kids' minds.

"What's college, Grandma?" Armond asked.

You know how it is with children; one question always leads to another. And before I knew it, Mama was being asked if she'd ever gone to college. That one question was loaded with insinuating implications.

In order to protect her, I answered, "Grandma is a Bruin." I said this proudly, recalling the day Aaron and I had attended her college graduation and cheered as she'd finally received that hard-earned diploma.

"That's right." Mama stood taller. "I graduated from UCLA! I was a little older than all my classmates, but your grandmother could still hold her own."

A little older. I chuckled to myself. By the time she finally found a way to finish her college education, she was far older than most of the other students, but she wasn't going to let a little thing like age deter her.

"I used to tell my classmates I was your mom's big sister. None of them believed I was old enough to be a grandmother," she teased. "Aaron, your mom brought you to my graduation. You were just a baby."

He hadn't even been a year old when my mother donned her cap and gown, but it had been important to her for her grandson to be in attendance, even though he was too young to remember the momentous occasion.

"Christa, I want my grandson to see me walk across the stage," she'd insisted. Her years of perseverance had finally earned her that degree, and we were all proud to celebrate her accomplishments. I obliged her and made sure that Aaron—aka Mr. President—was in attendance.

"I'm setting the example for my grandbabies, so they'll know that they can be anything they want to be. *Anything*," she whispered under her breath.

It was as if she were speaking to her past self. Informing her inner child that she had been the victor, defeating the obstacles that stood in her way—gender, race, class, and being *unwed*. She had battled my father, the Catholic Church, and even those suicidal voices, and she had lived to tell her grandchildren that they had the blood of survivors coursing through their veins. Along the way, she'd surely doubted her own abilities and strength, but in the end, she didn't let any of that stand in the way of her finally hearing the dean of the political science department at UCLA announce her name. If only they could have known what it had taken for her to get there.

In time, my mother slowly began to open up and share more about her own childhood and her relationship with my father. She admitted she'd had hopes of a white picket fence and a man who would love her for life, but those dreams had eluded her, through no fault of her own.

After hearing what she'd gone through, I understood why our relationship had been distant. It was hard for her to let down the walls she had built to protect herself from being hurt again, especially after her marriage with Norman had gone bad, leaving her without her babies. For the first time in years, she talked about my siblings, admitting that she'd never imagined that day at the motel would be the last time we would see them. All of these years later she was still haunted by the events that had led up to one of the worst moments in her life—the day she lost her two children. I could only imagine how painful it must have been to have to give up her babies because she couldn't afford to take care of them.

"They came and arrested me at my job and took me to jail." She explained that in the '70s women were not allowed to work and be on welfare when they were pregnant.

"I couldn't feed all of you on the meager government assistance I was receiving at that time. I did what I had to do."

Mama had concealed her pregnancy and was working and collecting welfare despite knowing that it was illegal. She had no choice but to allow Norman to take my brother and sister back to Alabama with him.

"I thought I would see them again. I just needed a little help," she said, with tears in her eyes. It was clear she was still suffering from the immeasurable loss. Abandonment and rejection were hard pills to swallow. She hadn't received the nurturing and love she'd needed to bring healing to her wounded soul. I couldn't fault her. It's impossible to give what you don't have. I knew that the only reason I was halfway sane was because I had discovered the love of the Heavenly Father, or shall I say, He'd discovered me. I was deeply loved by so many—my husband, my children, and a host of friends. Their love had helped to uproot the hurt I'd endured as a child.

My mother had spent many years believing the lie that she was to blame for the events that happened between her and my father. Believing that lie had caused her to close herself off from others, and more importantly, it had prevented her from being able to receive God's love. Or mine. Shame makes you feel unworthy of love, and that had hardened her in ways I still couldn't soften.

All I could do was to pray that He'd heal her heart and bring her the peace she needed. The peace I was experiencing. I believed God could also heal the things that were broken between us—it would just take time.

***

One afternoon, I received an unexpected phone call from my mother.

Without warning, she blurted out, "Christa, I found Hasan and Aisha! The courts have awarded me partial custody. . . well, maybe not quite *custody*, but the judge is letting them come to California for the summer. It's a start."

She went on to explain that she'd hired a private investigator to locate Norman, Hasan, and Aisha. Had I known she'd been looking for them, I would have prayed even harder—but, as usual, Mama had chosen to keep that a secret.

There you have it. Just like that, Hasan and Aisha were back in our lives after having been gone for thirteen years.

In that time, Norman had remarried. He, Hasan, Aisha, and his wife Barbara, were now living in Atlanta. Barbara and Norman had met and married when my siblings were very young. And she was the only Mama they knew.

An ugly court battle had taken place, and Hasan and Aisha had been ordered to visit Mama for the summer in California. They were now teenagers in high school. A lot of years had passed between us all. Sure, we shared the same blood, but in essence we were strangers.

I was nervous about how the visit was going to turn out.

"I'll bring them to Sacramento to visit you," Mama promised. "Just give me a few weeks to spend some time with them first." Then she hung up the phone.

I had conflicting emotions. My mother's announcement seemed to come out of the blue, and I hadn't had a chance to work through my feelings. Mama wasn't the only one who had missed them. I had missed my siblings too. I wanted to be there when they arrived, to welcome them back into our lives. We had so much to catch up on! And as usual I had too many questions. We had missed so much. Birthdays, holidays, sibling fights.

It was hard to believe that after all those years, we'd finally be reunited. From time to time, I had played the motel scene over again and again in my head. Was there anything I could have done that would have made things turn out differently that day? Had Norman gone away because of my childhood antics? Was I wrong for telling that little white lie that I was an only child? Of course, I knew that I *wasn't* an only child, but telling that story had always been a whole lot easier than explaining the truth when people would ask about brothers or sisters.

I dug through an old keepsake box and found the faded photos I'd kept of our little family. In the pictures, time was at a standstill. There was a photo of Hasan in a yellow footed onesie. In another photo, I was standing next to Mama as she held Aisha in her arms. She was just a few months old; a baby. Those images had become almost as grainy as my memory. But there we were, proof that all the love I'd felt for them had been real, after all.

I finally allowed myself to revisit the past, opening up the vault I had closed years earlier. Suddenly I was hurled back in time, laughing and playing with my little brother. Mama fed Aisha a bottle as she visited with her sisters. Hasan, with his big brown eyes, persuaded

Vicky and Fern to give him cookies. "Coo coo, Vi Vi, coo coo," which was baby talk for *Another cookie, please.*

His favorite toy was a red fire truck that my aunt had purchased for her son that Christmas. Hasan used those charming eyes again to persuade her to let him play with it instead. We weren't allowed to celebrate Christmas because of the whole Nation of Islam ordeal, so there were no trees or presents at our apartment. Besides, I'm sure that Mama wouldn't have been able to afford to purchase gifts, had we been allowed to celebrate.

My Aunt Vicky made up a silly song for Hasan. "Brother Norman had a baby, so, so . . ." During those absent years, she'd sometimes sing it, perhaps to hold onto the memories of better days.

Aisha was lucky; she had a song written about her too. *Isn't she lovely . . .* Stevie Wonder had penned the tune for his daughter, Aisha. Every time I heard it on the radio, I'd picture her as a baby, even though I knew she was much older now.

That night, I thought a lot about how things were going to change now that Hasan and Aisha were back in our lives. *Will they like me? Have Grandma Amelia and Aunt Jeanette talked about me or shown them pictures of me from that summer trip we all took down to Alabama?* One of Norman's brothers had taken a picture of Hasan, Norman, and me riding a horse. I tried to imagine what they looked like after all these years. Had they missed me as much as I'd missed them?

That Sunday, I shared my good news with my church family and asked them to pray.

Mama finally called me a few days after Hasan and Aisha arrived in LA. I could immediately tell that she was upset and that things were quickly unraveling. As she filled me in, she shared the details of their first week together in Los Angeles. They'd been spent reuniting with our extended family, and everyone was so excited. They'd all tried avoiding the elephant in the room—Norman. It was awkward.

My Aunt Vicky didn't want to know the full truth about Norman. She still held to the story that he'd stolen Mama's babies. As an adult, I realized that memories aren't always as accurate as we believe them to be. Truth is told as we have experienced it from our perspective. From Norman's vantage point, he hadn't stolen Hasan and Aisha, and they had never been in hiding. In his mind, he was simply doing what any good father would do, taking care of his children at all costs.

I was too young to understand why their marriage had been so tumultuous. I just knew their divorce had left me without the only father I'd known and separated me from my beloved siblings. I'm convinced that neither Norman nor my mother had expected the years of separation to pass so quickly, nor could they have imagined the amount of damage that would be left in so many hearts.

Inevitably, Hasan and Aisha began to ask her questions, questions Mama wasn't prepared to answer. Things between them got heated. Feeling backed into a corner, she reverted to her instinctual fight-or-flight mode, telling them her side of the story, and exposing the problems of her and Norman's marriage.

"Your father wasn't perfect," she said. "He had a terrible temper."

She didn't seem to understand that things were still too raw and painful for her to say such things. In our conversation a few weeks prior, I'd tried to dissuade her from discussing her troubles with Norman.

"Just try to get to know them and enjoy your time together. All the stuff between you and Norman should be kept there," I'd pleaded.

But she was desperate to defend herself, to explain why she'd left the marriage and to get them to understand that she'd never intended to leave her children.

"Mama, please," I begged. "You can't speak ill of their father. Whether fair or not, he's the one who's raised them and been there for them all their lives."

Sadly, my words fell on deaf ears. She needed to set the record straight, and nothing was going to stop her. Desperation can cause us to make rash decisions, and as her frustrations grew, she began to speak without a filter, saying things she'd later regret. Despite how badly my mother wanted to restore the lost years with her children, repairing their relationship wasn't going to happen overnight.

A few days before Hasan and Aisha's impending visit to Sacramento, the phone rang again. Instinctively, I knew that this call meant trouble, and I got a knot in the pit of my stomach.

I picked up the phone.

"Mama, what's wrong?"

"We got into a big fight," she said.

"Who, Mama? Who did you get into a fight with?" Supposing that she had gotten into a fight over the phone with Barbara and Norman, I told her that it was too soon to try to confront Norman.

"I'm not bringing them to see you. I'm putting them on a plane in the morning. They're going back to Atlanta!"

"What?!" My heart sank and broke at the same time. The fight had happened between Mama and my siblings. Things were worse than I had expected.

"Mama, please don't do this. Please," I begged. "We can work things out. Just calm down."

I had navigated dangerous waters like this before, but this time I felt like the captain of the *Titanic*. My head was barely above water. It felt too late to save this sinking ship. But God. . .

"God, help! Please don't let her send Hasan and Aisha home to Atlanta. I've waited so long to see them."

For the next twenty-four hours, all I could do was pray and wait and see how things would turn out. My mother was unpredictable when it came to matters of the heart. She had been abandoned by so many people in her life; she too had learned to be a runner. It didn't take much for her to cut you off. It had become her means of survival.

After many hours of my deep prayer, Mama finally reached out again.

"I'll be dropping your brother and sister off to you in Sacramento as we planned, but I'll be staying at a hotel for the weekend."

I released an immediate sigh of relief. "Thank you, Mama! Thank you!"

There was no way to know what had prompted her change of heart, but I felt certain my prayers hadn't hurt.

Now I was even more nervous about meeting up with Hasan and Aisha. I could only imagine how they were feeling. The entire ordeal had surely been overwhelming for us all. Mama literally dropped them off at my house. She didn't even come in to say hello. I opened the door and there they were, standing in front of me. I thought it would be awkward.

But then . . . another miracle!

My siblings and I hit it off immediately. It was almost as if we'd never been separated.

Perhaps it was Hasan's high-top fade haircut that gave him a few more inches, but I hadn't expected to meet such a grown young man—even taller than me!

Aisha was beautiful, the spitting image of our mother. I chuckled when I saw her feet—she, Mama, and I all had that same crooked index toe, the one that looked like it was running away from all the other toes on our feet. The three of us took time to compare our similarities, noting the freckles Hasan and I both shared. Even though

Aisha didn't have red hair or freckles, we looked alike in other ways. I wondered which side of the family Hasan had inherited his slender build from—that gene had certainly skipped over me.

Guss was wise enough to spend just the right amount of time with us. He popped in and out, so Hasan, Aisha, and I could catch up on the lost years. I think he knew how important it was for us to have time to reconnect. The three of us hung out all weekend, swimming at our apartment, eating pizza, and talking about their lives. I let them set the pace for our conversations. I was a proud big sister. We quickly discovered that we had many things in common.

Norman had long since left the Nation of Islam, and Aisha talked a lot about being raised in church and singing in the choir. I was especially thrilled to discover our shared love of music.

Hasan thought he was a comedian, and he told corny jokes all night. I felt it was my duty as the big sister to laugh at every one of them. He was very bright, like Mama. He'd already mapped out his future. He planned to become a doctor, which I knew would make mama proud. Yep, we were all Diane's children all right. She had given a piece of her genius to each of us, each in different forms.

We stayed up until dawn laughing with one another. They told me funny stories, like the time Hasan had duped Aisha into taking on his week of kitchen duties. She'd only agreed because she looked forward to collecting a little extra money. Each night Hasan made good on his promise to pay, but she didn't know that he'd been sneaking into her room and paying her out of her own stash!

"I told you I was the smartest one in the family," he said.

I laughed so hard my stomach hurt.

The pair bantered back and forth all weekend. Secretly, I imagined how different the sibling dynamics would have been if we had all been raised together. But as I thought more about how that life might have been, I began to realize that perhaps things were exactly as they should be. Statistics don't lie, and it seemed very likely that Hasan would not have survived growing up as a young man in The Jungle.

When Aisha called home, I got the chance to talk with Norman for the first time in years.

I also got to meet his wife, Barbara, by phone.

"Christa," she said, kindly. "Norman and I can't wait for you to come to Atlanta to spend time with us. Your brother and sister would be happy too. You have a big family here." She sounded excited.

Norman shared that he too had thought about me over the years and had often wondered how I was doing. It was a sweet moment, one that brought some healing to wounds I had long carried in my heart.

We kept in touch with each other by phone. A few years later, I surprised Hasan and Aisha by flying to Atlanta for Hasan's high school graduation. Barbara bought my plane ticket and made good on her promise to open up their home and to make me feel welcome. Aisha shrieked with delight as she came home from school to find me standing in their living room.

"It's my big sister!"

We jumped up and down in a long embrace. And I cried a little too.

"Come see my room," Aisha said. "Let's have a sleepover!"

She grabbed my suitcase, and off we went as if we'd never been apart.

That weekend, I got to see Grandma Amelia, Aunt Jeanette, and all the cousins I had met on my summer visit to Alabama so many years earlier. They were all in town for the graduation. I even got to meet Barbara's side of the family. I was happy to know that my brother and sister were so loved.

The night before I was to leave, Barbara took me up to her bedroom and sat me down on her bed. "I'm so glad you came to your brother's graduation, and I know how happy Hasan and Aisha are to have you back in their lives. You, Guss, and the kids have an open invitation to stay at our house anytime you want it."

My eyes welled with tears. She couldn't possibly know how much her kind invitation meant to me. In many ways, she had restored what had for too long been broken. She'd given me my family back.

"Thank You, Lord, for answering my prayers."

I didn't know if I could help save the relationship between Mama, Hasan, and Aisha, but I was grateful for the strong sibling bond between us.

Today, when asked if I have siblings, I answer the question without hesitation. "Yes! Yes, I do! I have a brother and sister. I'm the oldest."

Every time I answer, a wide smile stretches across my face, and I thank God that a little girl's dream to reconnect with her lost siblings all those years ago mattered to Him. He had reunited me with Hasan and Aisha, convincing me once again that anything is possible with God.

27

THE LETTER

One afternoon, while I was cooking yet another meal for my always-hungry brood of four, I decided that I would finally tend to the large pile of unopened mail that had been sitting on the kitchen table for a few weeks. It was a super busy season at work, which meant that I had neglected a few important tasks. I wasn't in too much of a hurry to spend my precious free time opening mail— most times it was either junk mail or bills. As I thumbed through the stack, I noticed a peculiar piece of mail. The postmark read Hermosa Beach, California. It appeared that it had been originally sent out several months prior, but for some reason it had gotten lost. I was fairly sure I didn't know anyone who lived in a beach town. I loved the beach and would have visited them often if I did! I could certainly use a vacation at the beach.

The only thing that caused me to consider giving this piece of mail my attention was the fact that it appeared to have been handwritten. Who'd be writing to me from Hermosa Beach, California? None of my people lived in a swanky area like that, or so I thought . . .

I helped the kids get started on their homework, and while they were busy practicing their spelling words for the week and working on math problems, I opened the letter.

Dear Christa,

I have made several attempts to contact you. My letters have all been returned unanswered. I'm not sure if you live at this address or if you are even interested in talking with me, but I thought I'd make one last attempt to reach you. I've included my phone number if you'd like to call me.

Kind Regards,
John Christenson

I sat there stunned for several minutes! After all these years, I was now holding a letter from my father in my hands. Did this mean that he wanted a relationship with me? What had changed his mind? Perhaps he'd been recently diagnosed with a terminal illness, and this was a final attempt to make amends before he went to meet his maker.

As I sat there at our family's kitchen table, holding a letter from the man who had abandoned my mother and me, a profound sense of sadness washed over me. It was the moment I had dreamed of when I was a little girl—at a time when little girls still held their daddy's hand as they cross the streets. Oh, how I'd longed for a father to read me bedtime stories and to chase the monsters away at night, especially when I would awaken from a bad dream. Where had he been when Mama and I were trapped in a reoccurring nightmare that wouldn't go away, even when the sun rose in the morning?

I wondered if he thought of me as he watched his daughter Chrisna go on her first date or learn to drive for the first time? These were the life events fathers were supposed to be present for. *So much precious time has already been lost—wasted!*

Of course, I wasn't a little girl anymore. Heck, I wasn't even a teenager. I was a married woman, with a family of my own. And against all odds, Guss and I had built a pretty good life for ourselves, minus a few bumps and scrapes here and there.

I held the letter in my trembling hands for what felt like hours, although I'm sure only a few minutes had passed. I'd waited for what seemed to me to be a lifetime. And now, this?

Can we recapture the lost years? Can he repair the damage that has been done to a little girl's heart? Am I finally going to be the recipient of my father's love?

Those questions raced through my mind. It was a lot to take in. Whatever my father's motivation, I had to give some serious thought to opening Pandora's box.

We had traveled down reconciliation road when I was a teenager and I'd ended up getting my heart broken. I still didn't know what had actually taken place between my mother and him. There were no answers to my long list of questions. So, I did what came naturally to me. I prayed.

"Why now? I'm finally at a point in my life where I am perfectly fine without my father. Should I just ignore his letter? The way he's always ignored me? Does he really think he can just waltz into my life after all these years?"

I continued pouring out my heart in prayer.

What might happen if I had the courage to respond? I wasn't sure if it was emotionally safe for me to get involved with my father again. It had taken years for me to get over the rejection I'd experienced at our first meeting. Finding my father, but never *actually* finding him . . . it had all been too painful.

But once again I heard a still small voice speaking, only this time I knew the voice well.

Christa, it's going to be okay. Remember I'm always with you.

***

A week or so later, I finally summoned the courage to call my father. I rehearsed our conversation in my head a few times before actually making the call.

Hello, is John there? This is his daughter, Christa.

That didn't sound right.

Uh, hello. May I speak to Mr. Christenson, please?

That sounded too formal.

I didn't feel prepared at all, but I was sure of one thing, *God had me* no matter what the outcome this time.

Those first few moments of our conversation were a blur. All I can remember is that it felt uncomfortable. Normally, it's easy for me to talk to people. I'm a friendly person who's never met a stranger. But this was different. This was my father—the man who had caused me so much hurt, pain, and disappointment.

In recent years, he had retired from being a school counselor and now spent a lot of time at home, alone. His health was failing him, but it wasn't anything terminal as I had imagined. I suppose the loneliness had prodded him to reach out. We made small talk. He asked a lot of questions about my family and about my life. We talked about my being married to Guss and how we had met one another in college. And of course, I talked a lot about our four exceptionally awesome kids. He also gave me updates about his wife, Yolanda, and their three children. I had almost forgotten that I had another half-sister.

This time something felt different. When he mentioned Chrisna, it didn't sting like it had when I was a teenager. I was surprised. With the precision of a skilled surgeon, God had performed spiritual surgery on my heart. The recovery process had been slower and more painful than I had hoped, but the reward was sweet. My conversations with my father were proof that God had provided tremendous healing in my soul.

Over the years, there were things God wouldn't let me avoid. Things I would have preferred to bury. But as much as I wanted to resist His promptings, to keep running from the pain—still do sometimes—He'd never let up.

Yes, God had held the door open for me, but I had to agree to walk through it. For years, I felt entitled to unforgiveness. I was sure that God would agree that I had a right to withhold forgiveness from my father. The thought of relinquishing control and forgiving him made me feel powerless. Who was going to keep the scorecard if I didn't?

It had been several years, but I could remember that watershed moment God had with me.

Christa, it's true that you've been hurt by the choices your mother and father have made. You have experienced many painful things in your life. But I'm offering you a new life. In order to have the life of freedom and healing that you've been searching for, you're going to have to choose to trust Me even more. You will have to surrender the bitterness that you want to hold onto. You will have to exchange your rights to anger, resentment, and unforgiveness for My grace. It's your choice. I'll never force you to do anything. You won't be able to forgive them without my help. Lean into Me.

I had chosen to do the hard thing back then and I'm glad I did. Forgiveness had been more for me than it was for them. Unforgiveness no longer held me in its clutches. I had been freed from its power over me.

***

Over the next several months, conversations with my father continued. He wanted to talk about spiritual matters. Under normal circumstances talking about politics or religion would be off the table, but God was really our only point of connection. It at least gave us some common ground.

"Are you Catholic?" he asked, with a hopeful tone in his voice.

For some strange reason, I didn't want to disappoint him. I guess most of us are looking for the approval of our parents, no matter the circumstances.

"No, I'm not Catholic. Guss and I are Protestants." I didn't know what the difference was between the two, except for the matter of going to a priest as the middle man. I was thankful that I didn't have to go to Pastor Hunt and air out all my dirty laundry in order to get forgiveness. I don't think either of us could have handled that.

He explained that he'd left the priesthood several years after I was born. He had gotten married to Yolanda, but he still held on to his Catholic roots. Faith still seemed to be important to him, as it was for me. He shared fond childhood memories of his family, particularly of his mother.

"As a child, my mother would sing as she hung the laundry out to dry," he said.

Is this where I got my love for singing? Was it passed down from my grandmother on my father's side?

I tried to imagine her in my mind as he talked. I hadn't given much thought about my father's side of the family. *Do they know about me?* I didn't have the courage to ask.

One afternoon, after having exhausted all the surface topics (the kids, Guss, my career, church, religion), with trepidation, my father finally broached the elephant in the room.

"How is your mother?"

How did he expect she would be? After having been left to raise a baby as a teenager all by herself in abject poverty? With no support? He had abandoned her. He had abandoned us.

I gave him a generic answer. "She's fine. She's an elementary school teacher now." *Truth was that she was never the same again after I was born.* Those words remained on the tip of my tongue but I didn't have the courage to speak them aloud to him.

The fact that he seemed to accept that response without asking for more, told me that he wasn't ready to face or hear the whole truth. Instead, he fumbled over his words, trying somehow to absolve himself, while never actually saying the words "I'm sorry."

I wasn't sure if he was truly sorry for the damage that he had done, for the pain that he had caused her, for shattering a family's faith, and for destroying a young woman whose future once swelled with so much promise.

In that moment, there was an unspoken understanding between us. What he couldn't know was that I had already forgiven him. God and I had wrestled through that painful process long before he had ever written *the letter*. There was nothing he could say to undo the past. And even if he had said the words I'd longed to hear, I'd learned long ago that nothing my father could do would make me whole.

Only God could do that.

We talked a few more times but it seemed the relationship between us had progressed as far as it could go. I'd made my peace with my father and decided that I could now close that chapter of my life.

He and I never spoke again. After chasing my father's love all those years, I finally realized that God's love, the love of my Heavenly Father, was more than enough.

28

THE PERFECT
ACCIDENT

For as long as I can remember, I've had an affinity for the summer months. The season tends to bring back memories of some of the happier times in my life. When I was a kid, my aunts, cousins, and I would often head to Santa Monica Beach with a cooler full of goodies and the family's hibachi grill in tow.

Alongside my cousins, I'd play in the ocean for hours, jumping waves and allowing the current to carry my body back to the shore. It was an escape from the realities of life. There, we weren't poor kids from the 'hood. We were just kids. The ocean always made me feel as if I didn't have a care in the world, and I was grateful my mother had taught me to swim as a little girl.

The summer of 2015 was no different. Guss and I took a quick trip to LA so that we could enjoy the ocean one last time before the summer's end. Our favorite spot was Manhattan Beach. As we held hands and walked the familiar stretch of sand, we relished the fact that this was our happy place. We loved everything about this beach. The people, the smell of the salty sea, and the sounds of the waves crashing against the shore. We didn't even mind that it just about took an act of God to get the sand off our feet. The beach had always been a place to regain sanity, to wash the rest of the world away.

Guss did his usual thing of pointing out all the houses that were for sale. He'd pull a flyer or two in an attempt to get me to buy in to his fantasy—vacationing at our Summer home on *The Strand,* which wasn't just any neighborhood. Every single one of these homes had amazing oceanfront views. It must have been amazing to have the Pacific Ocean as your front yard. *The Strand* was the crème de la crème of Manhattan Beach. The chances of Guss and I being able to afford a multimillion-dollar beachfront home there was as realistic as the MASH game mansion I had predicted I'd live in while waiting in that counselor's office back in junior high school. Guss and I both knew the exclusive neighborhood was out of reach, but it was fun to pretend.

After having come back down to reality, we caught up with Aunt Fern, Aunt Vicky, and my mother. Mama and I kept our conversation to our usual subject—the grandchildren. She was very proud of all of them, happily sharing in their accomplishments. Especially their college achievements.

My mama was giddy as she was telling me how she was bragging to her stylist about Armond and Arik. She said, "I let the whole shop know that *my grandsons* were two of the best football players in the state." She had no shame when it came to boasting about her grandchildren.

"Don't worry. I didn't leave my other two grand babies out. I told them all about my granddaughter and how she inherited her genius and passion for advocacy from me, and that my oldest grandson was a college graduate." Aaron had earned a business degree from San Francisco State University. "Good thing I planted those seeds when they were young," she smirked.

I nodded in agreement. I didn't mind sharing their success with her. After all, she had made the brave decision to give me life. If not for that choice, neither I nor my children would have the opportunity to make our impact.

The ride back to Sacramento was always bittersweet. Sacramento had become my home, but I did miss some of the familiarities of LA, especially the ocean. Thankfully, we only lived a few hours away. Guss and I immediately settled back into our work routines. For me, that meant I'd be helping to lead Women's Groups. I was also heading up the Music Department at my church.

I never imagined that the girl who had grown up without a religious bone in her body would one day become a pastor, especially since I'd been told that women couldn't hold that type of office in the church. *If only Antoine could see me now!*

One of the things I loved most about my job was the people I had the privilege of working with. It wasn't at all what people might expect of church. Ours was an eclectic group. On any given Sunday, you'd find people from every background worshipping together: Black, White, wealthy, not so wealthy, Boomers, Millennials. People from every walk of life imaginable were a part of our congregation. We'd all gather each week as a big, diverse family sharing common goals—loving God, one another, and serving our community. We had a saying at Midtown: "Not Church as Usual." The people were different and the gathering was much larger, but the message I had heard all those years ago when I'd first walked into Bethel was the same: God loves us! No matter who we are, where we come from, our status in life or lack thereof—God loves us. It's just that simple.

My birthday seemed to come around much faster that year—perhaps it was because I was pushing closer to the big five-o. I breathed a sigh of relief and relished the thought of holding on to the illusion of youth for 365 more days. For my forty-ninth birthday, we'd decided to celebrate by sharing a quiet dinner at a favorite local restaurant known for serving southern comfort food at its finest, which Guss and I regularly enjoyed. The owner greeted us with her usual exuberance, as she did all her regulars.

Minutes later, the most delectable spread filled our table—fried chicken, catfish, red beans and rice, honey cornbread, and a pitcher of sweet tea. Conversations and plans about the next year's festivities were already abuzz. Guss and the kids insisted we'd "do it up big" for my fiftieth. But for now, I was content to savor this simple evening—the joy of being with my beloved family.

I could hardly believe it myself. Not only would I be turning fifty the following year, but my husband and I would also be celebrating thirty years of marriage.

Where had the time gone? It felt like yesterday when I'd met the tall, slender basketball player with the warm smile and infectious sense of humor. His charming personality had won me over from the start. I'd almost forgotten about the fact that I'd been conned into going on our first date with the promise of *barbecue*. Almost thirty years later, I was still waiting on that dinner!

Amidst the conversations and laughter, my mind drifted back. So much had changed. Through the years, we had both added a few wrinkles and pounds, but we'd grown wiser too. Our relationship had weathered its share of storms since exchanging our marriage vows when I was just a few months shy of twenty. But in the midst of it all, we'd held tight to those promises to love one another, "For better or worse, in sickness and in health, until death do us part."

Thankfully, we were no longer starving college students, although I was still a student! After pressing "pause" on my college education to focus on our family, I'd recently decided to follow in Mama's footsteps. There I was in my forties, writing papers and taking mid-term exams, all while my kids were pursuing their own college degrees. It's funny how life repeats itself. On a hot Saturday afternoon in 2012, donning a black cap and gown, I strolled across the stage to accept my diploma. I had finally earned a degree in psychology, just like I had set out to do all those years prior.

That previous day, Armond graduated from USC. Those museum trips and pseudo college tours had made an impact. Mama was front and center at his graduation. "That's my grandson," she shouted as his name was called.

Armond teased me. "I beat you, Mom. It would have been embarrassing to tell my friends that my mom finished college before me."

Recently, I decided to pursue a master's degree in theology, a goal fully supported by my family. Still, starving students we were not. We had *moved on up!* Just like the Jeffersons. Neither Guss nor I had ever dreamed that we would have had such an incredible life. I'm certain that Guss had no idea that the hours he'd spent as a youth, poring over *Sports Illustrated* magazines and memorizing sports stats, would lead to a great career that he *absolutely loves.*

Although he didn't become the next Magic Johnson as he had hoped, training and developing other basketball players were equally fulfilling and rewarding for him. He'd discovered that he possessed a unique gift. His no-nonsense approach and innovative style of training had helped to push many players to the brink of greatness. Over the years he'd stuck with his passion, building solid relationships and developing a reputation as a broker of dreams, a true "basketball guru." Today, I'm proud to say that my husband is one of the most respected basketball trainers in the country. "He's helped countless players, at all levels, including the NBA." (Rob Benson SFGATE)

He's had the good fortune to work with the likes of Troy Hudson (LA Clippers, Magic, Timberwolves), Andre Miller (Cavaliers, Sacramento Kings), Bobby Jackson (Minnesota, Sacramento Kings), former NBA Rookie of the Year Mitch Richmond (Lakers, Sacramento Kings, Warriors), Matt Barnes (the UCLA superstar and the outspoken NBA standout), and countless others like him. In our years together, Guss has helped to lead a host of high-profile athletes to the top of their game.

Many of his clients have become a part of our extended family. I can still recall the day that Mike Wilks walked into our home for the first time. Mike had recently graduated from Rice University. He'd grown up in the toughest part of Milwaukee and had narrowly escaped becoming a statistic of gang violence himself. A strong mother, deep faith, and his natural talents on the basketball court had led him to a solid career in the NBA—playing with notable players such as Kevin Durant, LeBron James, and Kevin Garnett. In 2005, Mike played for the San Antonio Spurs alongside Tony Parker and Tim Duncan. That year they won the NBA Championship.

Oprah Winfrey once said, "Lots of people want to ride with you in a limo, but what you want is someone who will ride the bus with you when the limo breaks down." Mike was that kind of friend.

To date we remain close with Mike, his wife, Kim, and their two boys, Jo-Jo and Isaiah. They've since moved to Oklahoma where Mike has worked for the Oklahoma City Thunder for the past several years. He's a great friend, father, husband, and human. He's also a *survivor.*

Most of the players from that 1985 Sacramento Kings team have long since moved away, but we have maintained relationships with many of those guys. Guss and Tank still hang out regularly. Sadly, we've also lost a few friends along the way. Legendary players like Derek Smith, the consummate teammate with the "huge hands" and a "great touch," and Wayman Tisdale, the Grammy Award winning jazz musician with the infectious smile, were both gone too soon.

As I sat at the restaurant that night and began to reflect on the past, I couldn't help but be thankful for all the incredible people God had placed in our lives. I was even more grateful for Guss and our four children. My heart swelled with gratitude. Guss and I had been tremendously blessed.

Our lives were by no means perfect. We have had our fair share of struggles, still do. But the challenges have served to build fortitude, character, and a dependency on God. We've learned to value the things that are most important in life.

Somehow we managed to stay together for thirty-plus years, and out of that union came four amazing humans. Anyone who has ever been in a long-term relationship understands all that goes into it—it requires a whole lot of humility, patience, and forgiveness. We both had careers we loved, which has afforded us the opportunity to live with a sense of purpose. While sports has been an important aspect of our lives, faith has been our foundation and the focal point. It was the thing that has kept us grounded. Someone once said that we should give credit where credit is due. I am convinced that our family has been held together by the power of prayer. It had certainly been an answer to prayer that Arik and Armond had earned full-ride scholarships to play football for Division 1 colleges.

As the laughter spilled around me, I took a moment to thank God for my children. Aaron, our eldest son, was living in the Bay Area and working as a manager for a tech company. He remained the consummate big brother and protector of his younger siblings.

After having a great college football experience, we'd all been elated when in April of that year, Arik was drafted by the San Francisco 49ers. Having Arik play for a West Coast NFL team was unbelievable. We screamed with excitement when Roger Goodell, the NFL Commissioner, made the announcement:

"With the seventeenth pick of the 2015 draft, the San Francisco 49ers select Defensive Lineman Arik Armstead from the University of Oregon."

Aaron was especially happy, because living in the Bay Area meant that he could keep an eye on his baby brother. Another blessing!

But Arik hadn't been the only professional athlete in the family. It was Armond who inspired Arik to play football. Arik had always preferred basketball over football. But Armond had somehow convinced him that he could dominate on the football field as well. Turns out that he was right. After graduating from USC, Armond had the opportunity to play in the Canadian Football League (CFL) for the Toronto Argonauts. In 2012, they won the Gray Cup. It just so happened that it was the one-hundredth year celebration for the league, which made the win all the more special. That year, he was named a CFL All-Star and was named Defensive Lineman of the Year. He also had a short stint with the New England Patriots before retiring.

Our daughter, Alexis, hadn't chosen a path in sports, although she probably could have. To this day, she continues to taunt her brothers, reminding them that she still holds the record for the most quarterback sacks at their high school alma mater. Her sports accomplishments didn't quite make the official record books because it turned out they didn't recognize the stats from powderpuff football games. Go figure! But her dreams of impacting the lives of children have taken her to Washington DC; Lafayette, Louisiana; Kenya; and back to Northern California where she has worked with underserved youth while also pursuing a degree in Social Welfare and Public Policy at UC Berkeley.

We couldn't have been prouder of our children. They'd all grown up to become compassionate, loving individuals. I've prayed for them to be able to somehow make a difference—each in their own unique way. While I was proud of their accomplishments, it was even more gratifying for me to see them serving and caring for others.

Loud laughter brought my attention back to my delicious birthday feast.

"What were you thinking about?" Guss asked.

"Honestly, I am reflecting on all the things the Lord has done in our lives."

All those years ago, while kneeling in that tiny apartment bathroom, God had encouraged me to trust Him. I dared to do just that, and now here I was, thirty years later, surrounded by so much love and laughter, my heart could hardly hold all the joy. We had been the recipients of the goodness of God all right! Beyond anything I'd ever dared to imagine as a teen.

***

Exactly thirteen days after my birthday celebration, on Wednesday, September 14, 2015, I was awakened by the incessant chiming of my cell phone. Our family group chat messages for the day read:

"Happy Birthday, big bro."

"We love you, Aaron."

"Love You, Son."

The month of September is sweet because my mama, Aaron, and I, are all September babies. It had been Aaron's idea to start a family group chat, so that we could stay connected. Most times the postings are humorous and silly, depending on the happenings in the country. This particular morning, the messages were filled with love, admiration, and appreciation for our firstborn baby boy! I read the thread and then gave Aaron a call. It had become a tradition of mine to call the kids on their birthdays, to render them my own version of a singing telegram. Using my most creative motherly voice, I'd recount the details of day they were born.

"You may have grown taller than me, but you're still my baby," I said before breaking out into my version of the *Happy Birthday* song. It was a sweet, tender moment—at least for me.

That evening I was helping to host an event at the church. After the gathering had ended, a few of us lingered around to make sure everything was put back in order. Guss popped in to check on me before heading for home.

"I'm out. How long are you going to be?"

"We're almost done." I assured him. "I'll be home shortly."

He gave me that *quit-talking-and-come-on-home* look. He knew me well.

When he left, I turned back to the conversation we'd been having before he'd come in. That evening's message led to a deeper conversation about my past and some of the crazy stuff I'd done in my previous life.

"I can't picture you doing any of those things," one of my friends commented.

"Yeah, well that's because you didn't know me BG—before God," I said. "You only know the G-rated version of my life!"

Most of us go through life feeling as if we have to keep up the façade that we have it all together. We tend to hide, for fear that if people really knew us, they might not approve of us or worse, reject us.

Admittedly, I still wrestled with Imposter Syndrome—a *psychological occurrence in which an individual doubts their skills, talents, and even their accomplishments, and has internalized fear of being exposed as a fraud, despite the external evidence of one's ongoing success.* (Merriam Webster)

The conversation grew a little more serious, and the women seemed truly interested in hearing as much as I was willing to share. Although I lightened the tone with my sense of humor, I began to confess long-kept secrets about my early years. I told them about what life had been like growing up in The Jungle. For years, I had tucked many of those memories away. As the stories flowed, I was reminded of the desperation I had experienced as a teenager.

"Life had become so different for me in Sacramento," I admitted. "A mother, wife, and pastor. It's almost as if all those earlier experiences had happened to someone else." It felt as if I had lived two lives, drastically different from one other.

One of my friends looked at me and said, "Christa, you've got to tell your story. It could help people."

"Nah, nobody needs to hear all that," I said, shaking my head and returning my focus to the business at hand.

"But they do," another friend said, encouraging me to find a way to share my journey on a bigger scale. "It's a story of forgiveness, redemption, and overcoming. You can help people who are struggling."

I had hoped that by telling my story I could help to bring awareness and understanding and to help people to see through the lens of compassion, especially for the children who have had to grow up in similar circumstances as I have. The manner of our birth, the places we are born, and the families we are born into are not within our control.

They continued to nudge me to tell my story to a broader audience. I admitted that I had thought about the possibility of putting pen to paper all those years ago, just after we had gone on the *Phil Donahue Show*. But life got busy and the timing never seemed quite right. That night something began stirring in me. I couldn't shake the feeling that maybe it really was time to start opening up about my past. Maybe others could benefit from hearing about my journey toward forgiveness, reconciliation, and wholeness. God had certainly done miraculous healing in my life.

We soon said our goodbyes, and I headed home.

Then, just after I'd turned out of the church parking lot, *Wham!* My car started to spin violently. I lost time.

All. Went. Black.

When I came to, I was standing upright near the passenger side of my little Honda Accord. I slowly began to recall the moment of impact. When I saw the deployed air bags, broken windshield, and mangled mess resembling my car, I instinctively began checking myself for injuries.

Am I hurt? There didn't seem to be anything wrong with me, which was shocking, considering the condition of my vehicle.

How did I get out of the car without opening the driver's side door?

Did I climb over the center console and exit on the passenger side?

I couldn't remember.

My immediate thoughts turned to Guss. I scrambled around looking for my cellphone. No luck. *What am I going to do?* I sat down on the curb, trying to process the situation. Although I wasn't in pain, I was worried that I might have sustained internal injuries, or worse . . . that I might black out again.

Suddenly, a man appeared out of nowhere. I had seen plenty of movies where an angel visits a person at the scene of an accident right before he explains to them that they aren't actually alive anymore.

"Ma'am, are you all right?"

Is he a guardian angel? Am I dead?

"I've called 9-1-1, and they're on the way," he said, before moving quickly to check on the people in the other vehicle.

I hadn't even processed the fact that other people had been involved. I was numb and confused.

When he returned, I inquired about the people in the other vehicle. "Are they okay? Am I really okay?" My hands were shaking, and I was doing all I could to fight back tears.

I assumed this was how it felt to be in shock. Nothing made sense, as I tried to reason through the scene.

The man pointed out that my car had been thrown across several lanes and had spun around in the opposite direction. "I don't know how you avoided hitting those streetlights," he said. "Or the trees."

Obstacles stood all around me, including massive cement blocks supporting the freeway. Miraculously, my car had been gently guided to safety, and somehow I had managed to get out of the car, although I still couldn't figure out how I'd done that exactly.

"I'm not sure how, but it looks to me like you're okay," he replied.

With my voice quivering, I thanked the stranger for his help. "Could you please call my husband?"

When the kind man sat down next to me, I grabbed his arm and held on tight. As shock was wearing off, fear was settling in. I began to pray to God under my breath, but as I thought about how close I had come to death, my prayers grew louder.

"Thank You, God! Thank You for protecting me!" I prayed for several minutes and held even more tightly to the man's arm, as if we knew one another well.

"I was in my apartment watching TV, and I heard a loud crash. I came running out to see what happened," he explained.

At that moment, I knew that he wasn't an actual angel, but I'd still swear I saw wings. I was amazed by the kindness of this complete stranger. Another Good Samaritan, just like the one who'd saved my cousin Gary and me from rival gang members all those years ago.

By that time, other bystanders had begun to stop and offer help. *Where is Guss? Why isn't he here yet?*

"Please, can you try calling my husband for me again?" I rattled off his number to another passerby.

Guss finally arrived on the scene just as the paramedics were carrying me to the ambulance on a stretcher. Rushing toward me, his eyes were wide with worry.

"These have been the most terrifying thirty minutes of my life," he said. "I've driven up and down the neighborhood looking for you. The guy on the phone told me you were at Twenty-third and Broadway, not X street."

Guss hopped back into his car and followed the ambulance to the hospital, where emergency room doctors rushed to examine me—poking and prodding every inch of my body. Despite the mangled car, not a single bone was broken! My only apparent injury was a large gash on my head. I didn't even have a headache.

I joked with the medical team. "Apparently being hard-headed can have its benefits, after all."

Once the staff determined that my situation wasn't life threatening, they disappeared. It was *Déjà vu* all over again. There I was in the ER room, having narrowly escaped death, with just a few bumps and bruises. Guss arrived a few minutes later, still shaken.

Shortly afterward, my daughter Alexis arrived. Fearing the worst, Guss had also called Bob, a close friend of the family to meet him at the hospital. After having seen the pictures of my car, Bob and Alexis were surprised and thankful to find me sitting up in the ER talking and laughing. My daughter was the first one to break the news to me.

"Mom, now that I know you're okay, I need to tell you that you look like one of those characters in a scary movie. We need to clean you up some."

I had smacked my head pretty hard in the accident, but I wasn't aware that I had been bleeding. She helped me hobble down the hallway to the ladies' room, and we passed a priest praying with a family in one of the trauma rooms. In that instant, my entire life flashed before me, and I realized how quickly it could have all been gone. Never again would I have visited with my family members back in LA or hugged Mama. Never again would I have sung *Happy Birthday* to my children or told my husband how much I loved him.

The image of that priest represented nearly fifty years of a life that had been no accident after all. God had a plan for my life from the start even though the events that led to my conception were messy. The pregnancy, my mother's agonizing decision to keep me rather than give me up for adoption, and my struggle to find acceptance, belonging, and worth had been redeemed through God's love.

I wondered how things would have turned out differently, if my suicide attempt all those years earlier had been successful? What if those seizure pills had taken hold and sent me to an early grave?

We all know Father John Christenson should have never engaged in a relationship with his vulnerable young student, Diane, all those years ago, but if he hadn't . . . I wouldn't have been born. I would have never met Guss. Our four beautiful babies would have never entered this world. All their gifts and talents would have never been shared with the countless people whose lives they touch every day. God is able to redeem even the bleakest situations. I am a witness that He is able to take messes and turn them into messages of *hope*.

As I sat in that hospital bed, surrounded by the people I love most in this world, I realized that it wasn't only my own faith that had gotten us all to this point. Maybe, just maybe, all those prayers whispered in desperation by my mother—and even my grandparents and the ancestors before them—had not gone unanswered after all. Maybe it was a part of His divine plan to heal the wounds across generations. In His own time.

Yes, a lot of pain, suffering, grief, and loss could have been avoided if Father Chris had made a different choice when he violated his trusting student. But I was reminded of Psalm 139—the passage I had wrestled with all those years before:

> *Oh yes, you shaped me first inside, then out; you formed me in my mother's womb. I thank you, High God—you're breathtaking! Body and soul, I am marvelously made! I worship in adoration—what a creation! You know me inside and out, you know every bone in my body; You know exactly how I was made, bit by bit, how I was sculpted from nothing into something. Like an open book, you watched me grow from conception to birth; all the stages of my life were spread out before you, the days of my life all prepared before I'd even lived one day. Your thoughts—how rare, how beautiful! God, I'll never comprehend them! I couldn't even begin to count them— any more than I could count the sand of the sea. (The Message Paraphrase)*

God had been there at every stage of my life. Even in the times that were the darkest for me. He was there when I felt unworthy, unlovable, and so hopeless that I wanted to end my life. When I sat on the stage of the *Phil Donahue Show*, almost thirty years prior, I couldn't fathom being free from the stigma of being the illegitimate daughter of a Catholic priest. But God knew the wonderful things

He had in store for me all along. What a beautiful life it turned out to be in spite of how it all began. It's been a life filled with far more good than bad. And too much love to measure. Thankfully, I have discovered *the Sacred*, that which is *Holy* and *Divine*. We have *all* been created in His image and likeness and that makes us sacred.

On the journey to finding my earthly father, I discovered that my Heavenly Father had been there all along. He had never abandoned me. Yes, my earthly father had made some costly mistakes, choices that brought so much pain into many lives, but thanks to God, my true Father, I have found community, belonging, freedom, redemption, and a sense of worth and purpose. I have been able to forgive, which is no small feat, and to be forgiven. The journey doesn't stop here. There is still much for me to learn and areas where I am still growing. However, I'm not alone. God is with me and, for this, I am eternally grateful.

AFTERWORD

The car accident proved to be a wake-up call, reminding me that life could end at any moment without warning. It left me asking myself, *What will I do with the time I've been given?*

When I was a young college freshman plunged into the spotlight on *The Phil Donahue Show* all those years earlier, I wasn't yet ready to share my truths with the world. There were some things I needed to wrestle with and to be healed from. But after the car accident, my friends' words came back to me, encouraging me to share my story. In the weeks after the wreck, their suggestions kept surfacing, and I could no longer ignore that little voice inside of me that was urging me to *tell the truth*!

Finally, I understand why Mama needed her story to be heard, why she needed the world to acknowledge what had been done to her. Maybe it wasn't as much about justice and revenge as I had once believed. Maybe it was more about restoring her own self-worth, reclaiming her true self, and resurrecting that young innocent soul who'd been "crucified" for the simple act of offering love and devotion to the wrong kind of man.

From the moment my mother met Father Chris, a spiral of consequences followed until Mama had endured one hurt too many. Like a long chain of dominoes being toppled, she'd finally collapsed.

But through it all, she always loved me the best she could. And she has always loved my children too.

Today, I'm bravely peeling back the armor that kept me alive through the most dangerous seasons of my life. I'm sharing my story on my own terms now, not for anger or justice or revenge—that would only serve to destroy me in the end. Instead, I offer this truth to the world because I now know my story is just one of many. I believe there are others out there like me who need to know that they're not alone.

I hope to offer a lifeline of hope to those who are hurting, to those who are considering ending it all because you don't believe your life matters. I hope you hear me saying *don't give up*.

This book is for anyone who feels as if you don't belong. To anyone who believes you have nothing to offer, or that this world is far too cold and cruel and chaotic to survive with your soul intact.

It's for those who have experienced hardships, trauma, abandonment, and abuse in their lives and who are searching for a way to survive the unspeakable events life has thrown at them.

I'm also writing to those of you who have yet to discover the depth of God's love. You don't have to share my same experiences in order to know Him. He's been there all along in your life too. My hope is that within these pages, you would discover the light of God to illuminate your path, so that you can live the life that you are destined to live.

**Please note: Some names and places have been changed to protect the identity of certain people in this story. **

ACKNOWLEDGEMENTS

I am deeply grateful for the opportunity to share my story through this memoir. Writing a book is a challenging endeavor, and I am humbled to have accomplished this feat.

To all those who have supported me throughout this journey, I owe a debt of gratitude. Your encouragement, support, and prayers have sustained me through the painstaking, yet rewarding, process of putting my thoughts and experiences onto paper.

A friend shared that only a small percentage of people who aspire to write a book ever see their dream come to fruition. Without your unwavering support, I may have been among that vast majority who never took that critical first step toward publication.

So to my family— Guss, Aaron, Armond, Alexis, and Arik and to their spouses, I want to express my sincerest thanks. You have been my rock, my sounding board, and my inspiration. Without your encouragement, I would never have made it to this point. This memoir is as much your accomplishment as it is mine. Thank you for being with me every step of the way.

A special acknowledgment goes out to my best friend, Valorie Margaret Taylor, for helping this dream come to fruition. Thank you for encouraging me not to take a shortcut and for insisting that I tell my own story in my own words. Thank you for all the hours you dedicated to editing and helping me get the first draft of the manuscript completed. I couldn't have done it without you. I'm eternally grateful for our friendship and sisterhood. The time I spent with your family helped me survive those difficult adolescent years. Thank you for being the Ethel to my Lucy for over four decades and counting.

Thank you, Mama, for giving me life and for teaching me how to survive. Thank you for taking the kids on those summer field trips and for planting the seeds about the importance of college while they were young. Your legacy will live on in all of us.

To my cousins Nikki and Lisa, thank you for sharing your lives with me. Rest in peace, Gary.

Thank you to the Hunt family for showing me what healthy families look like. Also, thank you for teaching me about God in real and practical ways.

Thank you, Kira Bautista, for answering my calls, texts, and emails, for taking my photo for this book and other projects, for always sharing your creative expertise, and for helping to design the book cover. I owe you, girl.

Thank you, Chafie Fields, for introducing me to Tim Hoy at Wasserman. Tim, thank you for all the support you have given me— on the house.

Thank you, Jeanne Rodriguez, for your encouragement and for being a resource to me. We did it!

Thank you to Emily Wheatley and Lesley McDaniel for your insight and help editing this memoir.

I would like to express my gratitude to Efrem Smith and Chaplain Earl Smith for continuously encouraging me to get published. Your trailblazing efforts and inspirational leadership are greatly appreciated.

Thank you, Julie Cantrell. I owe you a debt of gratitude for all your help and for endorsing this memoir.

Thank you to Ann Kreis for your endorsement and support.

To my pastor and friends, Bob and Letty Balian, thank you for your friendship and for giving me the green light to follow my heart and dream.

Thank you to my Midtown Church family for all your love and support and for buying my book.

Thank you to the team at Redemption Press for helping to finally get this book published.

If I have have forgotten to acknowledge or to thank you please count it to my head and not my heart.

ABOUT THE AUTHOR

CHRISTA ARMSTEAD is an inspirational leader, author and speaker, the wife of Guss Armstead of *To The Hoop Basketball Services* and mother of Aaron, Armond, Alexis, and Arik Armstead of the San Francisco 49ers and the founder of Armstead Academic Project. Christa's commitment to supporting and helping others is evident in her body of work as a pastor and community advocate. Drawing on her own experience of pain and hardship, she has cultivated a deep well of compassion and sensitivity to the needs of others. Alongside her family and church community, Christa has worked tirelessly to empower the marginalized and those who have been forgotten or left behind. Her faith has been a constant source of strength and inspiration, enabling her to overcome personal challenges and to find freedom. Christa is passionate about sharing her journey of healing with the world, offering hope and guidance to those who are striving to break free themselves or to help others to be liberated.

Pictured left to right: Guss, Arik, Christa, Alexis, Aaron, and Armond

Pictured left to right: Aaron, Armond, Arik, Christa, Alexis, and Guss

Portions of the proceeds from this book will go to Armstead Academic Project (AAP), a non-profit organization founded in 2019 by Christa's son Arik Armstead and his wife, Dr. Melinda Armstead, MD. AAP is dedicated to ensuring every student, no matter their socioeconomic status, has direct access to the resources they need to thrive. To learn more about how you can support Education Equity and help to provide youth with positive spaces, tools, and academic support to unlock their potential and achieve their goals, visit armsteadproject.org.

Pictured left to right: Christa, Arik, and Guss.

CONNECT WITH CHRISTA

You can also connect with Christa by visiting her on social media:
Instagram: https://www.instagram.com/christa.armstead
Facebook: https://www.facebook.com/christa.armstead
Twitter: https://twitter.com/CArmstead916
Linkedin: https://www.linkedin.com/in/christa-armstead/

Christa Armstead

ORDER INFORMATION

To order additional copies of this book, please visit
www.redemption-press.com.
Also available at Christian bookstores, Amazon, and Barnes and Noble.

CPSIA information can be obtained
at www.ICGtesting.com
Printed in the USA
LVHW042204210723
753026LV00004B/763